Effective
Curriculum
for Underserved
Gifted Students

A CEC-TAG Educational Resource

Effective Curriculum

for Underserved Gifted Students

A CEC-TAG Educational Resource

Tamra Stambaugh, Ph.D.,
and Kimberley L. Chandler, Ph.D.

Series Editors
Cheryll M. Adams, Ph.D., Tracy L. Cross, Ph.D.,
Susan K. Johnsen, Ph.D., and Diane Montgomery, Ph.D.

PRUFROCK PRESS INC.
WACO, TEXAS

Library of Congress Cataloging-in-Publication Data

Stambaugh, Tamra.
 Effective curriculum for underserved gifted students : a CEC-TAG educational resource / by Tamra Stambaugh and Kimberley L. Chandler.
    p. cm.
Includes bibliographical references.
ISBN 978-1-59363-842-9 (pbk.)
1. Gifted children--Education--United States. 2. Children with social disabilities--Education--United States. 3. Children of minorities--Education--United States. 4. Curriculum planning--United States. I. Chandler, Kimberley L., 1961- II. Title.
 LC3993.9.S725 2012
 371.950973--dc23
                        2011030727

Prufrock Press Inc.
P.O. Box 8813
Waco, TX 76714-8813
Phone: (800) 998-2208
Fax: (800) 240-0333
http://www.prufrock.com

I hear and I forget.
I see and I remember.
I do and I understand.

—Confucius

Table of Contents

Preface

When examining the extant literature in gifted education, one can find numerous resources describing the characteristics of underserved students (i.e., those learners not traditionally identified in large numbers), the need to identify these students and to tailor the process in specific ways, and various curriculum and instructional modifications that may be beneficial to these children (Plucker, Callahan, & Tomchin, 2004; Shaunessy, Karnes, & Cobb, 2004). In addition, reports of research studies, particularly those funded by the Jacob K. Javits Gifted and Talented Students Education Act of 1988, have been published on the topic (Olszewski-Kubilius, 2006; VanTassel-Baska, Johnson, & Avery, 2002). There has not been, however, a comprehensive examination of recent studies regarding the efficacy of curriculum interventions with this target population.

The purpose of this publication is to provide a systematic examination of the curriculum interventions found to be effective with underserved gifted students, in order to derive common features. We then present a model based on the research that incorporates the elements of curriculum design and delivery that have been found to be essential for promoting the achievement of students from underserved gifted populations. This approach serves as the backdrop for establishing evidence-based recommendations for use by teachers, school counselors, educational leaders, researchers, professional developers, parents, and community members.

We discuss related topics of interest briefly to provide the reader with an overview of other areas that warrant attention regarding these students, such as intrapersonal skills, external persons of influence, and significant experiences. We also address assessment as applied to curriculum, instruction, and alternative identification methods found effective in special projects.

Appendix A includes several useful items for practitioners: (a) website addresses of organizations serving the needs of underserved gifted populations in some capacity and (b) website addresses of companies selling research-based curriculum resources that would be appropriate for use with these students. Appendix B includes an annotated bibliography of several key publications and books related to curriculum for underserved populations.

In order to address the needs of underserved gifted students effectively, it is essential to design and deliver curriculum interventions in specific ways. We present the key elements of such interventions so that practitioners will have an easy-to-use resource for directing their efforts. Many thanks are extended to the researchers, teachers, and administrators who have contributed both to this endeavor and to the growing body of literature that has informed this publication.

CHAPTER 1

The Elusive Nature of Defining Terms and Conceptions

"Working together, the school curriculum, families, and communities can enable positive, culturally consonant coping strategies and enhance self-efficacy in ways that acknowledge social realities while building the confidence to overcome them" (Kitano, 2007, p. 34). Curriculum modifications and the related actions that various stakeholders can take to address the needs of underserved gifted students most effectively are examined in this book. Both theoretical and empirical references to these curriculum-based interventions for enhancing the self-efficacy of underserved populations can be found in the literature. We summarize those references and delineate common themes, synthesize the themes in the form of a new model incorporating essential elements of curriculum design and delivery, and then use the information as the basis for a set of recommendations for practice. Although curriculum, instruction, and assessment are inextricably linked, the primary focus of this publication is on curriculum-based interventions targeted toward and found to be effective with underserved gifted populations.

Before examining curriculum interventions, we must establish who these students are, how relevant terms are being defined, and common misconceptions and conceptions about this unique population. Making distinctions about who these students are and what we assume versus what we know about them will help educators better plan curriculum and instructional opportunities suited to their students' needs.

WHO ARE GIFTED CLD LEARNERS?

Culturally and linguistically diverse (CLD) learners are any learners who may be underserved in a gifted program. Although the term *CLD learners* may have different meanings in different contexts, it is applied in this book as an all-encompassing term that includes any student whose culture and/or language is different from that of the majority culture in his or her school. Culture describes the values and practices of a given society or group, the culture of poverty, or the culture of an ethnic group in the United States. CLD learners comprise a large group of students who, although very different, also share some common characteristics. However, they differ in these characteristics just as much as they are alike. Additionally, CLD populations may demonstrate these characteristics in different ways from the dominant culture, sometimes in such a way that these characteristics may be perceived as negative. Some common characteristics include: high verbal ability in the native language, strong storytelling ability in the native language, strong critical thinking skills in the primary language, long attention span and ability to concentrate intensely, humor displayed through a unique use of language, and richness of imagery in ideas (New Mexico State Department of Education, 1994). It is important to understand that "giftedness, conceptualized as exceptionally high performance capability, is a characteristic of the individual as defined by the particular culture" (Kitano, 2010, p. 14). Therefore, some of the characteristics of CLD students are ones that teachers may not recognize, due to the cultural specificity. In some cultures, for instance, children are taught not to question authority; thus, it may appear that the child is not assertive in presenting his ideas to the teacher. Also, characteristics that we commonly consider traditional of giftedness may not be represented in CLD students in the same way. For example, risk-taking behavior is often considered a common characteristic of gifted students; for the CLD student, the degree of risk-taking will vary depending on the child's comfort with the situation based on her cultural background. School personnel must realize that CLD students will vary in their degree of acculturation to standardized testing and the expectations of schools (Kitano, 2010).

WHO ARE UNDERSERVED/ UNDERREPRESENTED POPULATIONS?

Underserved populations are commonly CLD learners. Specifically, this population includes groups of learners who have not traditionally been served in large numbers by gifted education programs. The underserved populations addressed in this book are CLD learners and children of poverty. Although underachieving and twice-exceptional students (e.g., those who are gifted and have learning disabilities) are considered to be underserved populations, they will not be discussed in this publication, as they are a primary focus of other books in this series. Underserved populations include both wealthy CLD learners of various ethnicities as well as learners of poverty, both in the majority or minority culture. It is difficult to distinguish between CLD learners who are also ethnically and racially diverse and those of poverty, as these conditions may be overlapping.

CLD students of poverty are sometimes referred to as disadvantaged, low-socioeconomic status (SES), or low-income students, and children of poverty. Disadvantaged students are children who qualify for free or reduced lunch according to the regulations of the Title I program, regardless of race or ethnicity. Typically, a Title I school has about 40% or more of its students living with families who qualify as low income under the United States Census's definitions.

KEY TERMS

Diversity refers to a classroom or school in which more than one culture or ethnicity is represented in significant numbers. A diverse gifted education program is one that accurately reflects the overall ethnic composition of the school population. The term diversity is one that is often used in the language of gifted education, in regards to attempting to represent the school population through the identified population.

Promising learners are students who show some evidence of advanced cognitive skills, but whose test scores and class performance need to be enhanced through special interventions in order to qualify for or have access to accelerated opportunities. This term indicates that the children have the potential to display advanced skills. In order to develop this potential, however, additional scaffolding of some type will be needed.

Multicultural education refers to the knowledge, dispositions, and skills that can help school personnel and students to become culturally competent in preparation for their work with diverse populations. Because the school population in many places has numerous cultural groups represented, teachers must begin to learn how to identify student strengths and weaknesses among students whose background may be different than their own. This is a significant and important undertaking, as the lack of a multicultural classroom can affect the achievement of gifted CLD students (Ford, Howard, Harris, & Tyson, 2000).

Gifted and talented children are those who by virtue of outstanding abilities are capable of high performance, as identified by professionally qualified persons. These are children who require differentiated educational programs and services beyond those normally provided by a regular school program in order to realize their contribution to self and society. Children capable of high performance include those with demonstrated achievement and/or potential ability in any one of the following areas:

- general intellectual ability,
- specific academic aptitude,
- creative or productive thinking,
- leadership ability,
- visual and performing arts, and
- psychomotor ability (Marland, 1972).

One emphasis of the Javits research in recent years has been on the most effective ways to identify CLD learners for gifted programs. Although it is beyond the scope of this book to describe appropriate identification procedures for CLD students in detail, it is essential to note that alternative methods must often be used and barriers to identification must be removed. Another book in this series focuses on this topic, as do various

NAGC resources including the monograph, *Overlooked Gems*, listed in Appendix B and available as a free download at http://www.nagc.org.

Terms related to how to best adjust both curriculum and instruction to CLD learners' needs also need some explanation. First, what is the difference between talent development of all learners versus actual service provisions? *Talent development* refers to any intervention that seeks to identify the potential in students and help them to become self-actualized so that they can realize their potential and make a contribution to society. Although talent development is an important construct in gifted education, the development of special gifts and talents of all students is also considered; however, for gifted learners—especially underrepresented CLD learners of various minority groups and of poverty—talent development is especially critical, as these learners need more opportunities to develop talent than those without these designations.

The curriculum for gifted CLD learners is critical, as will be discussed later in this book. *Curriculum* is the "reconstruction of knowledge and experience, systematically developed under the auspices of the school (or university), to enable the learner to increase his or her control of knowledge and experience" (Tanner & Tanner, as cited in Borland, 1989, p. 175). Curriculum materials are often developed with certain standards as a basis or utilize specific books. The curriculum interventions discussed in this book include both specific books that are prescriptive in nature as well as a set of standards and activities used by trained teachers. What then is the difference between curriculum and instruction? *Instruction* refers to the methods the teacher uses to deliver curriculum. The pedagogical strategies routinely used by teachers are examples of instruction. These may include but are not limited to: goal-setting strategies, grouping placements with differentiation, interest-based learning approaches, scaffolding, graphic organizers, and modeling. Scaffolding is a method of both breaking down accelerated content into lower to higher level thinking skills so that students can gain more knowledge and confidence, and providing more independence as students become comfortable with complex tasks. Scaffolding moves students from lower to higher level thinking and also from lesser to greater levels of independence in the completion of tasks.

Differentiated curriculum is curriculum that has been modified in some way in response to learner needs. For gifted students and for gifted CLD students, there are specific ways that curriculum must be differentiated. The type and degree of differentiation is usually based upon an assessment of the learner's readiness, interest, or learning style (Tomlinson, 2001). However, for gifted CLD learners, we recommend that differentiation be modified based on students' readiness first while taking into account the interests and learning styles of these students. Readiness should be the first consideration for CLD learners who lack access. This is the mechanism that guides differentiation and is used to determine learning goals and outcomes. Interests and learning styles of this unique population are used, not as a way to differentiate, but as a way to engage students in interacting with a curriculum that promotes higher level thinking skills based on ability or readiness.

MISCONCEPTIONS AND CONCEPTIONS ABOUT CLD LEARNERS

Research on the topic of CLD learners, especially those who are gifted, does not have the longevity or quantity of publications as do other topics in gifted education, such as acceleration and grouping. As such, along with the growing research in general education about these learners, there are many misconceptions and conceptions about the students that must be acknowledged in order to move forward with a discussion about curriculum and instruction.

MISCONCEPTIONS

It is important to dispel some of the common misconceptions about CLD students before discussing the major conceptions that will form the basis for this publication. These misconceptions are ones that may be held by teachers, administrators, counselors, and other school personnel. Practitioners must understand why these statements are misconceptions in order to see the strengths of CLD students and make appropriate educational decisions for this group. They are:

- *Misconception 1: CLD students are less intelligent than other students.* Although CLD students may show their talent in ways not normally measured by some of the more traditional assessments, they are not less able. Gifted students may be found in every ethnic and socioeconomic group. However, the interplay between environment and genetics may play a critical role in the realization of talent, thus limiting students in various ways.

- *Misconception 2: CLD students are always disadvantaged.* Many times the terms *poverty, ethnicity,* and *minority* are used in a way that connotes that all CLD students from minority ethnic groups are disadvantaged or poor. This is not the case. Many CLD students are wealthy or advantaged in other ways, such as access to social capital within a community.

- *Misconception 3: Parents of CLD students do not care about their children or school issues.* Most parents do care about their children's education and academic success. However, some parents of CLD students do not know how to advocate for their children or may find it culturally inappropriate to question the school faculty. In other instances, the competing obligations of family, school, and work inhibit the parents' visible support of their children at school functions. Additionally, the parents of these children may have had a bad experience in school themselves, and thus are reluctant to interact with school personnel.

- *Misconception 4: Certain ethnic groups tend to be stereotyped as being from low-socioeconomic settings.* Some ethnic groups report higher numbers of students who live in poverty than other groups, although not all CLD learners are from poverty. This is an important concept to remember. We cannot assume that just because students are from a certain ethnic group, they come from dire circumstances. However, when this interplay between poverty and ethnicity does exist, it is hard to determine whether poverty or ethnicity is a culprit for achievement or underachievement, thus making it difficult to generalize to specific populations.

- *Misconception 5: Curriculum should not be modified for CLD students; they need to adjust to the majority culture in order to succeed.* Appropriate education for all students links new content to previously learned ideas or a student's background or schema. Moreover, good teachers typically adjust curriculum and instruction based on students' readiness while considering their interests and learning styles. CLD students may have different interests, backgrounds, or ways of learning that must be accommodated in order for learning to take place. Although readiness varies with all students, appropriate pacing and exposure to higher level thinking skills can be beneficial.

Now that the major misconceptions have been addressed, what are the important conceptions about CLD learners within an educational framework of curriculum and instruction?

CONCEPTIONS

The major conceptions undergirding this book are comprised of two components: (a) the fundamental ideas about how and why curriculum must be differentiated for gifted and talented learners and (b) the major ideas that speak to the need for specialized interventions for underserved populations. The ideas about differentiation for gifted and talented students are commonly accepted in the field of gifted education, but they may not be familiar to teachers in regular education settings. Much of information about the need for and efficacy of specialized interventions for CLD students has been garnered through the Javits research projects described in this book.

Tanner and Tanner's definition of curriculum (as cited in Borland, 1989) emphasized how curriculum serves as a way for students to make sense of and use their knowledge and experience. Borland (1989) defined differentiated curricula as "modified courses of study designed to make the schools more responsive to the educational needs of these exceptional learners" (p. 171). Tomlinson (2001) echoed the issue of responsiveness to learner needs and described the elements of curriculum that could be differentiated: content, process, and products. Many of the elements of a defensible differentiated curriculum for gifted learners found in the current literature of the field are "recommended practices," which, according to Shore's (1988) definition, are suggestions based on the scholarly work of theorists but are not necessarily based on empirical research. Borland (1989) noted that although defining defensible curricula for the gifted is influenced by an individual's philosophy regarding the appropriate education of these learners, the key to defensibility is demonstrating the relationship between the students' exceptionalities and the features that make the curriculum differentiated. He stated that the minimum requirements for a curriculum for gifted learners must include: (a) agreement regarding what gifted students should learn beyond the core curriculum, (b) the existence of a scope and sequence to frame the knowledge and resulting instructional design, and (c) systematic and intentional alignment with the core curriculum. Once a framework is established based upon these requirements, then it is important to incorporate the following features: an emphasis on thinking processes, meaningful content, independent study, and accelerative options.

According to Maker (1982), the essential elements found in definitions of a differentiated curriculum are: (a) the unique characteristics of gifted learners, which forms the basis for the differentiation; (b) the inclusion of concepts of greater complexity or higher levels of abstraction; (c) an emphasis on the development of advanced thinking skills; and (d) the provision of materials or logistical arrangements to facilitate student growth. Focusing on learner needs as the driving force, Maker's list of characteristics of a differentiated curriculum includes: sophisticated content, an emphasis on higher level thinking skills, the development of quality products, and opportunities for independent study. Throughout the gifted education literature, the modifications espoused for differentiating curriculum for gifted students may be categorized as relating to content, process, product, learning environment, and affective concerns.

In her discussion of appropriately differentiated curriculum, VanTassel-Baska (1994) first emphasized three distinguishing characteristics of gifted learners: their ability to learn at faster rates than their peers, their ability to find and solve problems, and their ability to understand abstractions and make connections. She noted that these learner characteristics must be considered throughout the entire curriculum development and delivery process. These can be addressed through modifications of the content model, the process/product model, and the epistemological model to create a differentiated curriculum; these models include many of the features that Borland (1989) and Maker (1982) considered essential. VanTassel-Baska (2003) also outlined specific differentiation features that are essential for a curriculum to be considered appropriate for gifted learners: abstraction, acceleration, complexity, depth, challenge, and creativity. Each feature has descriptors that provide guidance for the types of appropriate modifications that must be made to meet the needs of these students.

Shore (1988) defined *recommended practices* as comprising "the considered advice of experts and persons actively involved in the field" (p. 9). In the preface to his list of recommended practices in gifted education, he noted that such interventions may be derived from empirical investigation but often are not; therefore, he would consider such practices to be *suggestions* for what teachers and parents should do. In a review of 98 books about gifted education, Shore and his colleagues developed lists of recommended practices in various strands, such as administration/advocacy, curriculum content/skills, and teaching strategies.

Since the time of Shore's examination (1988), other publications have provided information about the research base for various practices in gifted education. Robinson, Shore, and Enersen (2007) wrote a book in which they compiled the evidence base for 29 practices in gifted education. Plucker and Callahan (2008) edited a book examining the existing research base about 50 issues and practices. Both of these publications provide information that gives significant support for many of the curricular modifications promoted as being essential for differentiating for gifted students.

All of the ideas about how and why curriculum should be differentiated for the gifted relate to matching learner needs with specific interventions. In the nascent days of gifted education and even as late as 1988 when Shore conducted his review, substantial empirical evidence did not exist to support the claims of the theorists. Due to the Jacob K. Javits Gifted and Talented Students Education Act of 1988 in particular, there are now data that provide evidence of some effective curriculum interventions for producing achievement gains in gifted students. Because much of the focus of the Javits program in recent years was specifically on examining the efficacy of interventions with underserved populations, there are also data that comprise an evidence base about the curriculum interventions that are most appropriate when working with these children. Some of these ideas are different than the general recommendations discussed in the literature for the typical gifted population.

Applications of curriculum for gifted CLD learners. It has been well established that CLD learners are underrepresented in programs for the gifted (Boothe & Stanley, 2004; Ford, 1995; Van Tassel-Baska & Stambaugh, 2007a). This outcry about underrepresentation—especially for African American and Hispanic learners—has led to an increase in studies suggesting alternative and culturally fair methods of identification (Callahan, 2005; Lohman, 2009; Naglieri & Ford, 2003; Shaunessy et al., 2004). Consequently, in some schools a proportionate number of CLD students are admitted to gifted programs through alternate means (Van Tassel-Baska, 2010). Still, there is much to be done to increase these students' entry into and successful participation in gifted programs. Even though more gifted CLD students are placed in gifted programs than in previous decades, success in the program is not guaranteed. Many of these newly identified gifted students drop out of programs for the gifted because of (a) peer ridicule (Ford, 1995); (b) distance from their cultural peer group (Ford, 1995); and (c) lack of coherence between the student's identified strengths and the curriculum strategies and content of interest (Van Tassel-Baska, 2010). CLD students are more likely to drop out of gifted programs and also out of school, especially if they have less educated parents, are isolated from peers and the community, or do not participate in extracurricular activities beyond the school day (Renzulli & Park, 2000). Thus, a program of curriculum and instruction matched to CLD students' unique needs and abilities is of the utmost importance.

Applications in curriculum specific to CLD learners of poverty. What makes gifted CLD students of poverty less likely to be identified, and why does curriculum and instruction need to be modified for this group? There are two main categories of research on this topic: experiential and empirical. The experiential data most popularized in schools comes from the work of Payne (2001) and Slocumb and Payne (2000). Based on personal and observational experiences, Payne (2001) explained that students of poverty may be underrepresented because they (a) lack the social and financial capital typically enjoyed in middle- and upper-class society, (b) have less access to experiences that contribute to the environmental components of intelligence, and (c) must make tough decisions among competing priorities that distract them from education including survival, family expectations, care of siblings, or family financial support through afterschool jobs. Payne (2001) also noted that the language of students of poverty is less formal than their advantaged counterparts and, as such, students of poverty need to be taught formal ways of talking and writing. Promising students of poverty may be creative, tell great stories (although not always in a linear way), and struggle with setting goals, doing homework, and adhering to strict classroom structures (Slocumb & Payne, 2000). Although not all CLD students fit this description, educators should be aware of the variability among different groups and the impact poverty may play in conjunction with diversity.

A meta-analysis conducted by Sirin (2005) examined the impact of poverty on student achievement. Although his analysis did not disaggregate by ability or ethnicity, Sirin found that family provisions of resources, both physical and social, directly influenced student achievement. Moreover, the neighborhoods where families chose to live influenced the quality of the school and the curriculum opportunities for which a student had access, thus further hindering or enhancing social and academic capital for students of poverty. In addition, most schools of poverty have fewer qualified teachers and fewer offerings of advanced-level courses and curriculum opportunities (National Center for Education Statistics [NCES], 2006). According to an Education Trust (2005) report, school districts that host wealthier clientele spend approximately $907 more per student than their poorer counterparts; if the schools are comprised primarily of minority populations, then $614 less per student is spent than those schools with a majority population. Thus, a lack of resources in schools comprised of students who need the most perpetuates the potential lack of achievement gains among CLD learners.

Many CLD students also score significantly lower on state and national standardized achievement assessments, putting them further behind their peers (NCES, 2006). A two-fold approach to combat this inequity in gifted education is to (a) incorporate research-based alternative assessments that more effectively identify CLD learners and then (b) provide early curriculum interventions. Performance-based assessments (VanTassel-Baska, 2010; VanTassel-Baska et al., 2002), portfolio assessments based on students' performance on real-world tasks (Baum & Owen, 2004; Montgomery, 2001), certain nonverbal and verbal assessments (Canivez & Konold, 2001; Lohman, 2005; Mantzicopoulos, 2000; Naglieri & Ford, 2003; Shaunessy et al., 2004), and specific checklists and behavioral scale measures (e.g., Baldwin, 2007; Frasier, 1991; Johnsen & Ryser, 1994; Reid, Romanoff, Algozzine, & Udall, 2000; Worrell & Schaefer, 2004) have been successful in identifying more gifted CLD students than some of the traditional achievement and ability assessments—especially if these traditional measures are used as the sole determination for identification and access to programs.

Performance-based assessments are an especially good option for use with CLD students, both for access to programs and the evaluation of student learning. The purpose of performance-based testing is to determine the scope of knowledge a student has about a subject rather than testing the accuracy of responses to a specific set of questions. The benefit of performance-based assessments for CLD students is that they provide a value-added assessment measure that is targeted to specific areas of the curriculum.

Inclusionary methods such as the assessment of an entire grade level, not just those referred by teachers, also results in the identification of additional CLD students who are able to perform well in gifted programs (Bracken, VanTassel-Baska, Brown, & Feng, 2007; Jatko, 1995).

In order for students who are identified by less traditional measures to succeed, the curriculum must respond to alternate methods of identification as well as the unique needs of these students. The earlier the intervention and exposure to critical thinking tasks is provided, the more likely CLD students are to be successful (Campbell & Ramey, 1990) and to also be identified for gifted programs (Baldwin, 1994; Olszewski-Kubilius, 2006; Swanson, 2006; VanTassel-Baska, 2010). Briggs and Renzulli (2009) referred to the idea of "front-loading" as the need to scaffold instruction and nurture student abilities, thus facilitating the success of CLD students in gifted programs. Front-loading is a good metaphor for considering how we must think about our development and use of curriculum with this population, as it implies that certain things must be done deliberately in the conception and implementation of materials.

CHAPTER 2

Research-Based Curriculum and Instructional Strategies for CLD Learners

This chapter highlights both theoretical frameworks and quasi-experimental studies from the current literature on underrepresented populations. Before proceeding, a few caveats must be shared. First, most studies fail to disaggregate data so that comparisons of effects can be made between different types of CLD learners versus those of poverty. Many researchers provide the number of CLD students who participated in the study, but the data are not typically measured against outcome variables of significance by ethnicity and/or poverty, for example. This is understandable as these data are sometimes difficult to obtain due to privacy issues because school personnel are hesitant to release financial and ethnicity information. Additionally, in some studies, the sample sizes of participating diverse or low-SES students are too small for analyses when data are parceled. It is then difficult to untangle the overlap between poverty and ethnicity in intervention studies. Characteristics of underserved ethnic populations and students of poverty are so intertwined in the literature that it is difficult to decipher whether the findings of a study are due to ethnic and cultural issues, poverty, or both. Data from previous studies need to be disaggregated, if appropriate and available. Qualitative measures may also be conducted to follow up on quantitative findings about CLD learners.

QUASI-EXPERIMENTAL CURRICULUM/ INSTRUCTION INTERVENTIONS

The largest number of studies focused on CLD gifted learners in the field of gifted education targets identification issues (e.g., Ford, 1995; Joseph & Ford, 2006; VanTassel-Baska & Stambaugh, 2007a). Limited numbers of studies are available specific to a targeted minority group (e.g., Hébert & Beardsley, 2001), social-emotional needs (e.g., Shumow, 1997), or special programs and services (e.g., Robinson, Lanzi, Weinberg, Ramey, & Ramey, 2002) found to be effective for this special group. In general, large-scale curriculum studies focused on gifted students are limited (VanTassel-Baska, 2003) and almost nonexistent when considering the added dimension of poverty (VanTassel-Baska & Stambaugh, 2007a). Until the early 2000s, when federal Javits grants provided competitive funding for institutions to focus on scale-up curricula interventions for underrepresented populations, little empirical data on this topic were garnered through empirical studies with strong technical adequacy. Since then, curriculum units and the related efficacy studies have been published. Most of these studies focus primarily on students in Title I schools—schools that are comprised of a high majority of students on free or reduced lunch and/or who may be culturally diverse learners.

CURRICULUM STUDIES FOCUSED ON CLD LEARNERS

Studies from the Javits grants and other curriculum studies focused on CLD learners were perused and included in this chapter if they met the following criteria: (a) published results or curriculum within the past 10 years; (b) used quasi-experimental methodology (e.g., comparison and experimental group); (c) included a sample size of more than 450 students; (d) used an evidence-based conceptual framework from which to build knowledge and a strong curriculum; (e) reported significant differences between experimental and comparison groups (favoring the experimental group) on standardized achievement measures, not just perceptual scales; and (f) implemented the intervention during the regular school day.

After an extensive literature review, seven studies were identified that focused on this special population and also met the aforementioned criteria. These include Mentoring Mathematical Minds (M3), Project Athena, Project Breakthrough, the Jacob's Ladder Reading Comprehension Program, Project Clarion, Project U-STARS~Plus, and the Schoolwide Enrichment Model-Reading (SEM-R). Each of these projects will be described and compared in an effort to surmise patterns that can be replicated and used in general or gifted classrooms. Additional information about these projects and published curricula is found in Appendix A of this book.

Mentoring Mathematical Minds (M3). The focus of M3 was to develop and pilot advanced mathematics units for Title I students in grades 3–5. Gavin, Casa, Adelson, Carroll, and Sheffield (2009) used an evidence-based eclectic approach to the curriculum design, synthesizing knowledge from gifted education as well as best practices in the field of mathematics. The model highlights differentiated instructional practices based on students' level of readiness, acceleration followed by enrichment and extension of known concepts through problem episodes, and the cultivation of thinking and communicating like a mathematician (Gavin et al., 2009).

Professional development for teachers was also a primary feature of M3. Teachers were taught to help students make connections, to reason mathematically, and to create an environment conducive to learning mathematics. Twelve units were created and published. The units applied standards set forth by the National Council of Teachers of Mathematics (NCTM). Four units for each grade level were published, one in each of the following strands: algebra, data analysis and probability, geometry and measurement, and number and number sense (Gavin et al., 2009). The units highlighted the development of mathematical ideas, the use of mathematical language, problem-based activities or projects, verbal discourse, and the cultivation of a classroom environment that encourages learning. Differentiation strategies and activities were also incorporated into the curriculum and were emphasized in professional development sessions so that teachers could modify instruction through the use of "think beyond" cards for students with advanced experience and knowledge in the content area, as well as "hint" cards for those who needed even more scaffolding or experience to solve a problem.

Pre- and post-curriculum-based assessments were administered to monitor student achievement and adjust learning as needed for individuals and student groups. Students exposed to the curriculum performed significantly better on the Iowa Tests of Basic Skills (ITBS) in mathematical concepts and estimation. There were also significant and important differences in open-ended responses explaining mathematical thinking, favoring the experimental group. Gavin et al. (2009) concluded, "the results of this intervention suggest that curriculum units that are concept-based, that are accelerated and enriched, and that encourage students to behave similar to practicing mathematicians contribute to students' mathematical achievement" (p. 200). An example of a problem and follow-up questions is listed in Figure 1.

Project Athena. This longitudinal study utilizing The College of William and Mary curriculum units in language arts focused on the impact of critical thinking and reading comprehension scaffolding on students in Title I schools, positing gains in both areas for students who used the curriculum (Bracken et al., 2007). The curriculum, intended for students in grades 3–5 (*Journeys and Destinations*, *Literary Reflections*, and *Autobiographies*), incorporated graphic organizers to aid students in persuasive writing, literary analysis, and vocabulary development. Students who were introduced to the persuasive writing graphic organizer in particular (see Figure 2) showed significant gains in their ability to communicate in writing by formulating arguments, justifying ideas, and elaborating upon responses.

Teacher professional development focused on advanced processes and questioning to develop literary analysis skills through the use of advanced reading selections, oral discourse, and overarching macro concepts such as change. Teacher modeling of both literary analysis skills and persuasive writing through the use of the embedded graphic organizers was emphasized. Pre- and post-curriculum-based assessments in literary analysis and persuasive writing were included and discussed as an impetus to differentiate instruction for students based on their scores. Student choice in research and novel study was also a key component to help students plan and monitor their learning over time.

A New Discovery

Back at the dig, you have just found another tablet. It seems to have a list of characters on it with drawings that look like some type of stone counters. See if you can figure out what it all means.

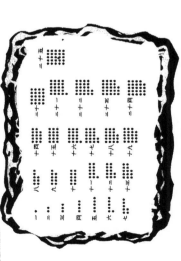

Also scratched on the other side of the tablet are some other characters that appear to be numerals. They look like the following:

四十五

三百一十八

八百二十七

二千四百一十六

Can you figure out the value of each of these numerals?

HINT CARDS — Hint Cards — A Mysterious Number System

HINT CARDS · HC
Which ways can you sort the information you have to look for patterns?
• MYSTERIOUS NUMBER SYSTEM •

HINT CARDS · HC
What does the 2 represent in 21?
What does the 1 represent in 21?
• MYSTERIOUS NUMBER SYSTEM •

HINT CARDS · HC
How do we write 21 in expanded notation?
• MYSTERIOUS NUMBER SYSTEM •

HINT CARDS · HC
How might expanded notation fit into the Chinese system?
• MYSTERIOUS NUMBER SYSTEM •

Figure 1. Moli stone example. From *Unraveling the Mystery of the Moli Stone: Place Value and Numeration* (pp. 61, 191), by M. K. Gavin, S. Chapin, J. Dailey, and L. Sheffield, 2006, Dubuque, IA: Kendall Hunt. Copyright 2006 by Kendall Hunt. Reprinted with permission.

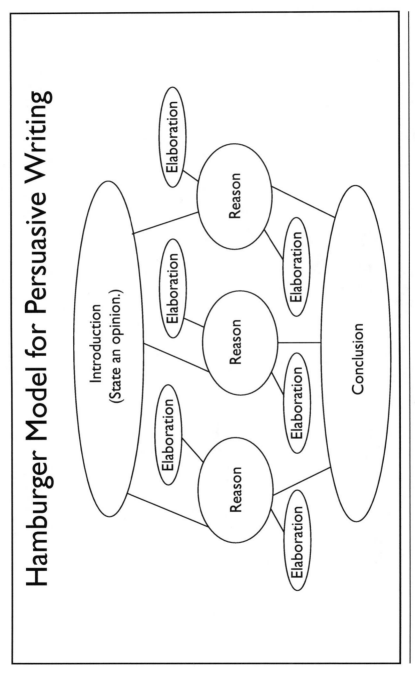

Figure 2. Hamburger persuasive writing model. From *Guide to Teaching a Language Arts Curriculum for High-Ability Learners* (p. 53), by Center for Gifted Education, 1999, Williamsburg, VA: Author. Copyright 1999 by Center for Gifted Education. Reprinted with permission.

The experimental teachers who used this curriculum in their classroom showed significant gains in their incorporation of critical and creative thinking, measured using a teacher rating scale, when compared to their colleagues (VanTassel-Baska et al., 2008). Moreover, students in this project showed significant and moderate gains in reading comprehension and in critical thinking after continued exposure to the various units (VanTassel-Baska et al., 2008). The most significant gains were made by non-Hispanic Whites, followed by African American students and then Hispanics (Bracken et al., 2007).

Project Breakthrough. Another study using The College of William and Mary science and language arts units also showed promise with more than 1,000 low-income and minority students in South Carolina. Swanson (2006) provided professional development on content-specific thinking models used in the units and encouraged teacher use of the models over 3 years. Selected William and Mary units in science and language arts were used as starting points, and teachers were encouraged to create their own units. Pre- and posttest data were collected using the Metropolitan Achievement Test (MAT) and the South Carolina State Assessment. The achievement scores of minority and low-income students who participated in the project were significantly higher than their nonparticipating counterparts. The key features of this project included teacher professional development, deliberate instruction about thinking skills and habits of the discipline, and the incorporation of open-ended questions and activities that promoted educational discourse.

Specifically, the use of problem-based learning episodes was infused into the curriculum as a way to promote critical thinking and engagement. One such science example (see Figure 3) shows a real-world situation in which students must work through an issue to learn more about electricity and create their own recreational center given specific requirements. This situation is used as a way to engage students, create an experience for them, and guide their learning throughout the unit to include student-generated questions, self-regulation, and goal setting.

Jacob's Ladder Reading Comprehension Program. The Jacob's Ladder Reading Comprehension Program (VanTassel-Baska & Stambaugh, 2009a, 2009b) was written for students in grades 3–5 to promote critical thinking and literary analysis skills and has since been

---

Initial Problem Statement

You are a newly hired employee for the local power company. Your first assignment after completing the company's orientation program is to work as part of a team that has been asked to design a recreational complex in the center of town. This project is backed by both federal and state funding. Your role is to ensure that power (electricity) requirements are planned appropriately and are adequate for the new complex. The complex will serve the needs of all community groups including senior citizens and special needs individuals. You must also design a comprehensive backup plan for the complex. Your training in college stressed city management and planning, not electricity.

Figure 3. Electricity City problem-based scenario. From *Electricity City: Student Pack* (p. 13), by College of William and Mary, Center for Gifted Education, 2007, Dubuque, IA: Kendall Hunt. Copyright 2007 by College of William and Mary, Center for Gifted Education. Reprinted with permission.

---

expanded to grades 2–9. The supplemental program provides short reading passages, poems, and nonfiction selections with guided questions in the form of skill set ladders. Each ladder focuses on a different literary analysis task and specific thinking skills. An example of a nonfiction piece and two ladder sets is shown in Figure 4. Note that the ladders focus on different thinking skills. Students are taught oral discourse through teacher modeling and questioning techniques. Different thinking "ladders," used as graphic organizers, are included in the program. Students metaphorically climb the ladder and move from lower to higher level questions as they build upon previously learned knowledge and skills. The program's conceptual framework is derived from Paul's (1990) Reasoning Model; the program is differentiated by skill set and ladder to better meet the needs of a variety of learners.

Pre- and postassessments are also incorporated within the Jacob's Ladder program to match students' abilities to specific thinking ladders. Teachers can then be more deliberate about tailoring students' needs and strengths to specific activities.

The teacher professional development component is key to the program implementation. A focus of the training is on the unique needs of students of poverty and how to ask open-ended questions, model Socratic

Name: _____ Date: _____

The Gettysburg Address
By Abraham Lincoln

Four score and seven years ago our fathers brought forth on this continent, a new nation, conceived in Liberty, and dedicated to the proposition that all men are created equal.

Now we are engaged in a great civil war, testing whether that nation, or any nation so conceived and so dedicated, can long endure. We are met on a great battlefield of that war. We have come to dedicate a portion of that field, as a final resting place for those who here gave their lives that that nation might live. It is altogether fitting and proper that we should do this.

But, in a larger sense, we can not dedicate—we can not consecrate—we can not hallow—this ground. The brave men, living and dead, who struggled here, have consecrated it, far above our poor power to add or detract. The world will little note, nor long remember what we say here, but it can never forget what they did here. It is for us the living, rather, to be dedicated here to the unfinished work which they who fought here have thus far so nobly advanced. It is rather for us to be here dedicated to the great task remaining before us—that from these honored dead we take increased devotion to that cause for which they gave the last full measure of devotion—that we here highly resolve that these dead shall not have died in vain—that this nation, under God, shall have a new birth of freedom—and that government of the people, by the people, for the people, shall not perish from the earth.

Figure 4. Jacob's Ladder example. From *Jacob's Ladder Reading Comprehension Program: Level 3* (pp. 42–44), by J. VanTassel-Baska and T. Stambaugh, 2009, Waco, TX: Prufrock Press. Copyright 2009 by Center for Gifted Education. Reprinted with permission.

Name: _____   Date: _____

Theme/Concept

C3

What does Lincoln's address say about the concept of liberty?

Inference

C2

What inferences can you make about Lincoln's hopes for the future of the United States? What evidence supports your answer?

Literary Elements

C1

How does Lincoln characterize the soldiers who died during the Battle of Gettysburg? Support your answer.

THE GETTYSBURG ADDRESS

Figure 4, continued.

Name: _____ Date: _____

Creative Synthesis

D3

Pretend you are an interested party from the audience (e.g., mother, father, sibling of a soldier; a soldier; a congressional leader; the secretary of war) who has just heard the Gettysburg Address. How would you react to the message of Lincoln's speech? Create a reaction to the Gettysburg Address.

Summarizing

D2

In three sentences or less, summarize the message Lincoln is trying to convey to the American people.

Paraphrasing

D1

In your own words, paraphrase Lincoln's statement, "It is for us the living, rather, to be dedicated here to the unfinished work which they who fought here have thus far so nobly advanced."

THE GETTYSBURG ADDRESS

Figure 4, continued.

seminars, and promote literary analysis skills and critical thinking. Pre- and post-curriculum-based assessments are used to guide instruction and to aid teachers in the selection of appropriate skill ladders and story sets for student practice. Data show that CLD students of poverty who were introduced to the program significantly outperformed the comparison group in reading comprehension and critical thinking, with moderate gains (Stambaugh, 2007a).

Project Clarion. The curricular goal of Project Clarion was to develop and pilot advanced-level curriculum in science for primary students in Title I schools, grades K–3. Eight curriculum units (*Water Works, Budding Botanists, Dig It, What's the Matter?, How the Sun Makes Our Day, Invitation to Invent, Survive and Thrive,* and *Weather Reporter*) were designed based on the Integrated Curriculum Model framework (VanTassel-Baska, 1986). Each unit framework incorporated advanced processes focused on helping students think like a scientist (i.e., problem-based learning episodes and scientific investigations), conceptual understanding of macro concepts such as change or systems, and accelerated content knowledge. Pre- and postassessments in each of these areas were used to measure growth and plan ongoing instruction.

Standardized assessments in science and critical thinking were also administered to the comparison and experimental groups. Students exposed to the curriculum showed slight gains on both the Metropolitan Achievement Test (MAT) in science and the Test of Critical Thinking (TCT; VanTassel-Baska & Stambaugh, 2007b). Statistically significant gains were made in scientific investigation for students in grades 2 and 3 after being exposed to the Wheel of Scientific Investigation, a scaffolding organizer (see Figure 5) to model habits of the discipline, question generation, and experimentation and discussion (VanTassel-Baska & Stambaugh, 2008). This model serves as a backdrop for the teaching of expertise within a scientific field and encourages curiosity, advanced scientific processing, and communication skills.

Project U-STARS-Plus. Project U-STARS-Plus (Using Science Talents & Abilities to Recognize Students: Promoting Learning for Underrepresented Students) focused on increasing the identification numbers of "at-potential" primary-aged students in Title I schools. Through this project, professional development was provided to help

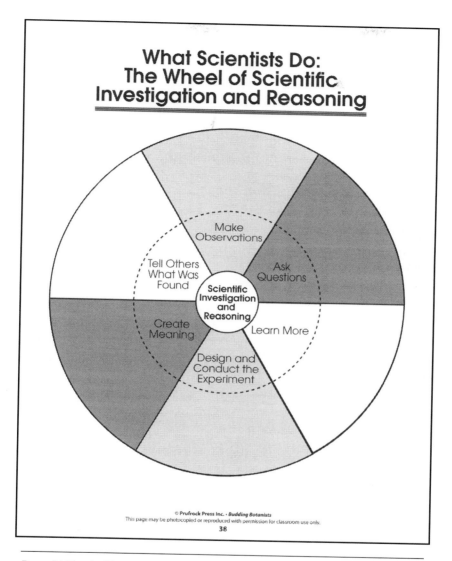

Figure 5. Wheel of Scientific Investigation. From *Budding Botanists* (p. 38), by Center for Gifted Education, 2010, Waco, TX: Prufrock Press. Copyright 2010 by Center for Gifted Education. Reprinted with permission.

teachers create appropriately challenging high-end learning experiences for their students, to practice mechanisms for observing and possibly identifying potentially gifted students from disadvantaged populations, and to provide a classroom climate that enhances discovery and learning (Coleman, 2007). Alternative checklists were used, resulting in increased numbers of students identified from culturally diverse backgrounds (FPG Child Development Institute, 2010). The teachers learned instructional strategies (e.g., curriculum compacting, questioning, tiered assignments) to solicit appropriate higher level thinking skills and behaviors within the classroom and focused on scientific inquiry to provide engagement and exploration that emphasizes conceptual thinking instead of memorization.

A noteworthy feature of this project is the involvement of parents and families in their child's education. Although other projects listed in this chapter incorporated homework extensions and activities into their curriculum, Project U-STARS~Plus is the only program that focused explicitly on the involvement and education of parents through a variety of means including workshops, orientation sessions, conferences, and parent nights. In addition, family packets were sent home so that parents could support what was being taught in the classroom through engaging activities and experiments.

Teacher resource lessons were also created to help teachers match instruction to student needs, incorporate high-end learning, and teach students to make interdisciplinary connections in an engaging way. A sample activity (see Figure 6) shows how lower level to higher level thinking skills were scaffolded using Bloom's taxonomy and scientific inquiry activities. Note that both science and language arts were incorporated in engaging ways to encourage student learning of varying ability and interest levels.

Schools that participated in the project showed higher achievement scores on their statewide assessments in reading and science than nonparticipating schools (FPG Child Development Institute, 2010). In addition, teachers reported that their students were more excited about learning and evidenced increased critical thinking behaviors (Coleman, 2007). An independent study of the project also cited Project U-STARS~Plus as

---

The Very Hungry Caterpillar Example: Language Arts/Science

➤ Knowledge: List things that the caterpillar ate when hungry.
➤ Comprehension: Describe each state of the butterfly's life.
➤ Application: Describe what would happen to you if you only ate junk food.
➤ Analysis: Compare and contrast the stages of the butterfly.
➤ Synthesis: Explain the relationship between the caterpillar and the butterfly.
➤ Evaluation: Describe which stage of the butterfly you like the most and why.

Figure 6. Question scaffolding for U-STARS~Plus. From *Rejecting the "At-Risk" Stereotype: Project U-STARS~Plus Helps Kids "At-Potential"* (p. 2), by FPG Child Development Institute, 2010, Chapel Hill, NC, Author. Copyright 2010 by FPG Child Development Institute. Reprinted with permission.

---

a promising practice for closing the achievement gap among promising students of poverty (Coleman, 2007).

Schoolwide Enrichment Model–Reading (SEM-R). The SEM-R project is an instructional strategy model focused on students in grades 3–5. The goal of SEM-R is to scaffold reading instruction based on students' choice and readiness levels and to develop reading skills through teacher-guided discussion and oral communication (Reis et al., 2007). Three phases of the project ensued, including remediation and interest-based reading selections, teacher-guided discussion groups, and students' goal setting and regulation of their own independent reading. During phase one, teachers read aloud to students with high-interest books, provided scaffolding in thinking questions, and led book discussions within a variety of genres. Bookmarks were created based on student interest and skills to guide students' development of literary discussion using their interest-based books. An example of a character analysis bookmark is shown in Figure 7. Note the open-ended questions and links to the text and student as part of the scaffolding and interest process.

Phase two focused on guiding students' reading based on their individual reading levels and interests. Differentiation of reading levels, teacher conferencing, and subsequent instruction were included with the main goal of helping students begin to self-regulate their learning by providing time for appropriate behavior engagement and guidance, helping

Characterization Bookmark

What gift would you like to give the main character and why?

Illustrate some of the similarities between two or more main characters.

How might you rewrite the story to include one of your friends as the main character?

If you were the author, what further events, episodes, or discoveries would you have the main character participate in?

Figure 7. SEM-R bookmark example. Retrieved from http://www.gifted.uconn.edu/SEMR/bookmarks.pdf. Adapted with permission.

students set individual reading goals, and providing cognitive strategies to help students become better readers (Zimmerman, 1990). The final phase, phase three, permitted students to self-select books and projects of choice.

Student attitudes toward reading were measured with the Elementary Reading Attitude Scale (Wigfield, 1997), which was administered to project participants and a comparison group. Students in the experimental group reported significantly higher satisfaction with reading and spent more time actively reading than their counterparts. The differences between the two groups were large. Students in the experimental group also scored significantly higher on a reading fluency assessment (passage reading with measured work speed and accuracy) and on a standardized reading comprehension test (Iowa Tests of Basic Skills Reading Comprehension subtest), with a small but significant effect size (Reis et al., 2007).

When examined together, the comprehensive findings of these research studies provide meaningful information educators can use when adapting or planning curriculum for CLD learners. Chapter 3 discusses the common features found across the studies and provides suggestions for planning and teaching this special group of gifted learners.

Before moving to Chapter 3, two additional models should be considered: multicultural education and Ruby Payne's work focused on students of poverty. Although not empirically based, these have been popularized in schools that serve large populations of CLD learners and/ or students of poverty and merit discussion.

THE ROLE OF MULTICULTURAL EDUCATION RELATIVE TO CLD STUDENTS' INSTRUCTION

Multicultural education is included in many reform models. However, little empirical research can be found on the effectiveness of such educational approaches on student achievement, especially for students who are gifted and CLD. The large-scale curriculum studies previously discussed did not incorporate multicultural education in a formal way but showed respect for students' backgrounds through the use of scaffolding, solicitation of multiple perspectives, respect for varied ideas, and student choice—all components of a respectful educational environment, especially for gifted CLD learners.

Banks (1997) saw multicultural education reform as a way to create equity among various ethnic groups. He identified five different dimensions of multicultural education: content integration, knowledge construction processes, an equity pedagogy, prejudice reduction, and an empowering school and social structure (Banks, 2004). First, content integration incorporates sublevels of knowledge and skills that teachers integrate into the curriculum as they provide examples from different cultures. The knowledge construction processes dimension focuses on the ways in which a teacher integrates different perspectives into a curriculum. An equity pedagogy ensures that instructional strategies are used in a way that is fair to all learners. For example, Banks (1997) cited research suggesting that cooperative learning environments are more conducive to achievement gains for African American and Hispanic students when compared to competitive environments. Thus, teachers should consider how their classroom is structured to better meet the needs of a variety of learners' characteristics.

The fourth dimension, prejudice reduction, is used to promote accurate information and reduce biases that may be perpetuated by different cultural groups. Banks (1997) alleged that some of the widely used curricula in schools promote false stereotypes about certain cultures and social groups. Teachers need to be aware of these inaccuracies and counter them with more appropriate resources and examples (unless, of course, these are primary documents used to solicit discussion about the context of the day). Specifically, teachers need to be cautious of using photos or reading passages that promote negative stereotypes and instead incorporate accurate cultural examples and positive role models as part of the curriculum. Finally, Banks's fifth dimension is that of empowerment of the school and social structure. This dimension is more systemic and engages schools in making decisions and policies that include and welcome diverse opinions, ideas, and cultures. Each of Banks's dimensions involves sublevels of understanding that teachers can use and apply to their teaching and curriculum.

Ford and Harris (1999) and more recently Ford (2011) combined Banks's content integration and knowledge construction sublevels with Bloom's taxonomy to create a template for teachers to focus on not only cultural awareness in their classroom but also higher level thinking skills. Figure 8 provides an example of the template with explanations of each cell. Note that the top of the chart applies Bloom's taxonomy objectives

	Knowledge	Comprehension	Application	Analysis	Synthesis	Evaluation
Contributions	Students are taught and know facts about cultural artifacts, events, groups, and other cultural elements.	Students show an understanding of information about cultural artifacts, groups, and so forth.	Students are asked to and can apply information learned on cultural artifacts, events, and so forth.	Students are taught to and can analyze (e.g. compare and contrast) information about cultural artifacts, groups, and so forth.	Students are required to and can create a new product from the information on cultural artifacts, groups, and so forth.	Students are taught to and can evaluate facts and information based on cultural artifacts, groups, and so forth.
Additive	Students are taught and know concepts and themes about cultural groups.	Students are taught and can understand cultural concepts and themes.	Students are required to and can apply information learned about cultural concepts and themes.	Students are taught to and can analyze important cultural concepts and themes.	Students are asked to and can synthesize important information on cultural concepts and themes.	Students are taught to and can critique cultural concepts and themes.
Transformation	Students are given information on important cultural elements, groups, and so forth, and can understand this information from different perspectives.	Students are taught to understand and can demonstrate an understanding of important cultural concepts and themes from different perspectives.	Students are asked to and can apply their understanding of important concepts and themes from different perspectives.	Students are taught to and can examine important cultural concepts and themes from more than one perspective.	Students are required to and can create a product based on their new perspective or the perspective of another group.	Students are taught to and can evaluate or judge important cultural concepts and themes from different viewpoints (e.g., racially and culturally different groups).
Social Action	Based on information on cultural artifacts, students make recommendations for social action.	Based on their understanding of important concepts and themes, students make recommendations for social action.	Students are asked to and can apply their understanding of important social and cultural issues; they make recommendations for and take action on these issues.	Students are required to and can analyze social and cultural issues from different perspectives; they take action on these issues.	Students create a plan of action to address a social and cultural issue(s); they seek important social change.	Students critique important social and cultural issues and seek to make national and/or international change.

Note. Based on the models of Banks (culturally responsive) and Bloom (thinking skills). Actions taken on the social action level can range from immediate and small scale (classroom and school level) to moderate (community and regional level) to large scale (state, national, and international levels). Likewise, students can make recommendations for action or actually take social action.

Figure 8. Bloom-Banks model. From *Multicultural Gifted Education* (2nd ed., p. 116), by D. Y. Ford, 2011, Waco, TX: Prufrock Press. Copyright 2011 by Prufrock Press. Reprinted with permission.

and the side of the chart applies a subset of the Banks's multicultural model. The template is divided into four quadrants following left to right and top to bottom. The top left quadrant shows lower level thinking and basic multicultural awareness; the top right quadrant couples higher level thinking skills with more basic cultural awareness activities; the bottom left quadrant highlights lower level thinking skills but more advanced levels of cultural awareness; and the bottom right quadrant models the most sophisticated levels of thinking and multicultural awareness to solicit social action. Ideally, teachers would aim to focus on the bottom right quadrant, scaffolding or differentiating the various quadrants as appropriate.

This model can be used to highlight cultural diversity, to focus on multiple perspectives, and to differentiate instruction using the various quadrants as differentiated aspects to incorporate lower and higher level aspects of multicultural issues and cognitive levels. Although no research has been conducted using this model, it combines two widely accepted frameworks and may be used to activate change and cultural awareness while also building critical thinking skills.

PAYNE'S FRAMEWORK FOR UNDERSTANDING POVERTY

Another model, Payne's framework for understanding poverty, is an instructional strategy approach highly popularized in schools, although her work comes with much criticism from the academic community (Bomer, Dworin, May, & Semingson, 2008; Gorski, 2005). Payne noted that her framework is naturalistic and inquiry-based, derived from her years of living in an area that experienced generational poverty. Payne (2001) argued that poverty is its own complex culture that includes more than just lack of finances and encompasses complicated belief systems and values not necessarily embraced by middle-class schools.

The term "framework" is misleading. Basically, this model emphasizes stakeholder awareness of the culture of poverty and highlights the characteristics and mindsets of the different types of poverty before applying specific strategies to help these students achieve. Payne's ideas and strategies are extrapolated from the educational and school change research and include basic pedagogical principles. Payne (2001) explained that learners of poverty, regardless of race or ethnicity, need to be taught specific formal language used in schools and also need targeted and specific instruction in basic cognitive strategies that other students take for granted (e.g., comparing and contrasting). She also notes the importance of role models and other support systems as part of a holistic approach to student learning.

According to Payne's website (http://www.ahaprocess.com), a national quasi-experimental research study was conducted and verified by outside sources, although only research briefs were included and no peer-reviewed journal articles could be found. Findings suggest that schools who incorporated Payne's framework showed significant gains in students' achievement in mathematics and language arts. School systems not included in the study posted similar results and credited the framework as the impetus for positive schoolwide change and increased achievement. Many educators find Payne's approach informative to their teaching as they better understand the unique characteristics of students of poverty and as such are better equipped to provide appropriate instructional strategies for them (e.g., graphic organizers, cooperative learning, the teaching of basic skills and language).

Educators are encouraged to use or modify evidence-based models instead of highly popularized models. However, these two models in particular have been widely acclaimed based on experiential data and are important to know so that one can be informed of research-based versus popular, experience-based models, strategies, and curricula. With such limited teaching time and increasing information available, we must be good consumers of resources—especially for those who are underserved.

CHAPTER 3

Common Features of Effective CLD Curriculum

The intent of this book is not to market or sell curriculum but to focus on the empirically supported features of effective curriculum for CLD students that can be incorporated into a general classroom setting, especially for those districts that do not have the resources or freedom to self-select or purchase specific curricula. This chapter highlights patterns that emerged from an analysis of the successes of the previously discussed research-based projects in Chapter 2. These patterns can be applied to classroom instructional practices, differentiation, and curriculum development or enhancement for CLD learners.

Eight specific patterns emerged across the projects and are synthesized for practical application (Stambaugh, 2009):

1. *Scaffold instruction through the use of graphic organizers and the teaching of thinking skills.* All of the curriculum projects incorporated some form of scaffolding for student learning. Scaffolding was evident in three ways: moving from lower level to higher level thinking skills, transitioning from less to more independence of student learning, and incorporating deliberate curricular and instructional pacing. Although the curriculum varied in terms of how scaffolding was incorporated, all curricula were created with the assumption that CLD students could work at higher levels of thinking and independence, although more time may be necessary to achieve this goal. M3 provided this scaffolding through the use of hint and think beyond cards, and Project Clarion and

Project Athena focused on graphic organizers that divided the higher level thinking tasks into smaller parts. Jacob's Ladder and U-STARS~Plus deliberately moved students from lower level to higher level skills while adjusting the individual pace at which students learned the tasks, and SEM-R incorporated activities to move students to more independent reading through differentiated task demands and teacher guidance.

2. *Emphasize the development of potential rather than remediation of skills.* High expectations of students, when coupled with advanced task demands and scaffolding, produce higher gains in CLD students than a focus on remedial skills. A key underlying assumption of each project was that CLD students could learn to think and perform at higher levels than their counterparts if provided ongoing exposure to higher level thinking skills, advanced content, and scaffolding. Unfortunately, many CLD classrooms, especially those in Title I schools, use remedial curricula that focus on rote tasks void of exposure to higher level thinking skills (Tivnan & Hemphill, 2005). Far too many educators incorrectly assume that CLD students are not capable of performing at or beyond grade level given unpleasant environmental factors and thereby seldom provide the opportunity for high-level work, especially in reading (Taylor, Pearson, Clark, & Walpole, 2000). This becomes a self-fulfilling prophecy as students who are rarely exposed to advanced material and have little possibility of engaging in accelerated activities are not going to learn how to work at high levels of achievement because of this lack of exposure. The curriculum interventions discussed in this book deliberately focused less on basics and remediation and more on exposure to gifted education pedagogy and advanced content. Guiding school district philosophy from an orientation of students who are "at risk" to considering them "at potential" has great merit and success (Coleman, Coltrane, Harradine, & Timmons, 2007).

3. *Focus on teacher modeling of both oral and written communication of the discipline.* The habits of the discipline are a constant theme throughout each project. Students are taught not only how to think like a practicing professional in the discipline, but also how

to communicate ideas in a formal way, applying the language of the discipline both in writing and orally. This is an important skill to be taught to students of poverty, who sometimes perform better on nonverbal versus verbal tasks (Naglieri & Ford, 2003) and may need to be taught formal ways to communicate effectively (Slocumb & Payne, 2000). Project M3 encouraged students to provide written explanations of how they arrived at a solution to a problem or to talk through how to solve a problem using mathematical vocabulary. Each of the language arts projects emphasized oral discussion of literary text through teacher modeling, open-ended questions, and small-group discussion with teacher modeling. Project Athena also focused on the use of graphic organizers to enhance students' articulation of ideas through persuasive writing models and oral presentations, while the Jacob's Ladder program provided response stems for students to begin group discussion. Similarly, SEM-R provided bookmarks with enrichment questions for teacher- and student-led discussions. The science projects focused on how to report and record collected data and write about the scientific methodology employed. All four of the projects related to this pattern showed significant results in the area of writing or articulating ideas, many times with the highest effect size within the project.

4. *Provide targeted professional development to teachers.* Teachers play a critical role in CLD students' learning. The importance of ongoing and extensive professional development must be emphasized, including the inclusion of modules related to the characteristics and needs of CLD students. Briggs (2003) reported that the effectiveness of interventions with CLD students was related to teacher readiness to assume the responsibility needed to maximize the impact of the interventions. A review of the Javits studies indicated teachers were not only able to identify more CLD students as promising, but, upon conclusion of the projects, also reported more comfort with applying accelerated curriculum or modified instructional strategies to enhance instruction for promising CLD learners. Many of the study researchers also reported that teachers were concerned that their students might

not be able to perform at the advanced levels intended by the researchers and the project curriculum. Upon conclusion of the studies, teachers reported that when these students were given the opportunity to work at advanced levels with scaffolding, they performed beyond expectations. In most of the studies, teachers also reported enhanced discussion of topics and student excitement about learning as positive, unanticipated results.

5. *Create opportunities for engagement including real-world problem solving and student choice.* One of the possible disadvantages of being a CLD learner is that typical experiences often enjoyed by the majority of learners may not be accessible to CLD learners. Because these students come from varied backgrounds, the curriculum must be relevant to a variety of students' needs and experiences. Each of the projects detailed above addressed the issue of relevance by embedding open-ended problem-solving opportunities and student choice. For example, M3 scaffolded instruction for student learning and then provided a mini-problem-based episode or experience for students to apply their new learning in a relevant way. (Review Figure 1 for an example.) The language arts curriculum projects incorporated real-world opportunities through student-selected books, open-ended questions for discussion, and issue-based research opportunities. In science, mini-problem-based episodes were used as a hook for future unit teaching and planned scientific investigations.

In Project Clarion, specifically, students were encouraged to create their own questions for investigation so they could practice applying the scientific method. Mini-problem-based episodes relevant to their school situation were also used to encourage student engagement, create an experience not otherwise encountered, and practice problem-solving skills. For example, a second-grade problem-based episode from *What's the Matter?* provides a letter from the principal explaining that her office has been quite warm and the ocean water she brought home as a souvenir from a vacation and displayed in the office, is now missing. Students are challenged to determine a scientific explanation for what happened to the water. Through redesigning the case and examining artifacts presented by the teacher and principal, students learn about evaporation, conduct experiments to test their hypotheses, and recreate what might have happened. This scenario allows for students to solve a relevant problem, engage in a scientific discussion with adults, and learn about evaporation and features of ocean water. Note that an experience was created instead of assumed or ignored.

6. *Incorporate student goal setting and self-monitoring.* Two of the projects explicitly applied goal setting for students. SEM-R was the most deliberate about this feature, asking students to become partners in their own learning by setting personal goals for the number of minutes to be spent independently reading. The increase in reading time favoring the experimental group was one of the most significant effects in the project. The Project Athena curriculum also incorporated goal setting and monitoring through long-term assignments and planned research projects. Two additional projects (M3 and Jacob's Ladder) incorporated self-monitoring by designing an environment where students could think like a mathematician or a literary analyst—emphasizing that professionals may take several days to solve a problem or discuss an idea. This idea of self-monitoring and goal setting provides a way to enhance social and emotional needs in the lives of CLD learners through a cognitive task demand.

7. *Use curriculum-based performance measures to modify instruction and measure progress.* Five of the projects (M3, Breakthrough, Athena, Clarion, and Jacob's Ladder) provided pre- and post-curriculum-based assessments to be used as a guide for student differentiation and to measure growth linked to instruction. Specifically, teachers administered a preassessment and used the data collected as a guide to homogeneously group students, provide targeted instruction (either accelerated or remedial), and reassess to measure growth gains. Students could become partners in their learning and track the progress they made so that a sense of efficacy could be built. This gave teachers a baseline to show that even though some students may not show great gains on state achievement assessments, they are still learning advanced

skills and content. Students in the experimental group showed significant and substantial gains on the pre- and postcurriculum assessments in all projects, even though some of these students did not perform as well on standardized assessments.

8. *Place effective curriculum in the hands of trained teachers.* Two of the projects incorporated strategy-based approaches (U-STARS~PLUS and SEM-R) instead of a more formal and prescribed curriculum. The projects that incorporated a prescribed curriculum (M3, Breakthrough, Athena, and Clarion) showed larger student achievement gains than the two projects that used strategy-based approaches. Although more research needs to be conducted on this topic, it appears that placing a prescriptive curriculum in the hands of trained teachers produces higher effect sizes in student achievement and teacher change than the teaching of instructional strategies without the accompaniment of curriculum. Other studies in the field support the idea that the teaching of strategies does not produce lasting effects (Westberg, Archambault, Dobyns, & Salvin, 1993; Westberg & Daoust, 2004).

CHAPTER 4

Factors That Impact Gifted CLD Learners' Responses to Curriculum and Instruction

Although curriculum is important, it is not the end in itself. Other factors also contribute to the success of CLD students. These factors are generally categorized as being external or internal. External factors focus on access: access to individuals or mentors within a discipline and access to special programs or activities that can enhance learning. Internal factors include the psychosocial aspects such as self-concept, efficacy, and motivation. Each are discussed below in more detail.

EXTERNAL FACTORS THAT CONTRIBUTE TO CLD STUDENT ACHIEVEMENT

ACCESS TO SPECIAL PROGRAMS AND SERVICES BEYOND THE SCHOOL DAY

The use of leisure time is a defining factor in student achievement and career paths during the lifespan (Csikszentmihalyi, Rathunde, & Whalen, 1993). Students who talk with adults, read during their spare time, and focus their attention toward educational endeavors and enrichment instead of watching television or working a part-time job are more likely to achieve at high levels during and beyond their school career. Afterschool programs, in particular, are an effective and efficient way for schools to provide enriched and accelerated services to students from disadvantaged groups. Extending the school day for at-risk populations helps these students focus on organizational skills, language building, homework skills, and socialization. Schools benefit by enjoying higher achievement scores; parents can enjoy the benefit of school-based, structured childcare, if needed; and students gain important educational skills. Advancement Via Individual Achievement (AVID) is one example of a structured afterschool program that has shown promising results for at-risk students. Although AVID was not designed for high-ability students, effects for all ability levels involved in the program are reported as positive. Specifically, students who participate in AVID show higher overall achievement than their counterparts and are more likely to enroll in advanced courses in high school and apply to college when compared to the national averages (Gira, 2007).

Talent search models are another effective service provided beyond the school day. Talent searches target high-ability learners and encourage participation in accelerated or enriched opportunities on weekends or during the summer. Out-of-level assessments (e.g., administering the SAT or ACT to seventh graders) are used to identify talented students. However, some programs offer alternative means for CLD students to be identified if they do not have access to out-of-level assessments (e.g., Northwestern Center for Talented Development, Vanderbilt Programs for Talented Youth). Unlike afterschool programs that may be more easily accessible, participation in talent search programs relies upon student application, family provision of transportation, and financial obligations, although need-based scholarships are typically available. Thus, fewer gifted CLD students will or are able to take advantage of such programs. Like general school-based gifted programs, CLD students are underrepresented in summer talent search programs (Olszewski-Kubilius & Lee, 2004). If CLD students do participate in a summer or Saturday accelerated program, they seldom return for a second summer, even if they are quite successful in the program (Worrell, Szarko, & Gabelko, 2001). Woods (2006) studied variables that impact retention in summer enrichment programs, especially for African American and Hispanic populations, and found that students were more likely to return each year if they began attending the program earlier in their school career and possessed advanced reasoning and language skills. Students whose mothers were the head of household were more likely to drop out of such programs.

When gifted CLD students maintain involvement in talent search opportunities, the results are quite positive. These students are more likely to apply to more selective universities (Olszewski-Kubilius, 2006; Sosniak & Gabelko, 2008), develop stronger peer and content mentor relationships (Johnsen, Feuerbacher, & Witte, 2007), and enroll in advanced math and science courses in high school—especially if provided early exposure and ongoing support (Olszewski-Kubilius, 2006).

Targeted counseling also makes a difference in accelerated summer programs. Brewer (2005) studied first-generation CLD college students who attended a summer talent search program. These students were provided educational and career counseling as part of their experience. As a result, they were more likely to enroll in postsecondary opportunities than their nonparticipating counterparts. This evidence suggests that targeted counseling and mentoring is necessary for retention and the future learning trajectory of CLD students.

ACCESS TO KEY INDIVIDUALS

Influential individuals such as teachers, content experts, counselors, clergy, or other key persons can significantly impact the lives of CLD learners (Stambaugh, 2007b). Each of these individuals could be considered a mentor for these students. Teachers, in particular, are the gatekeepers of identification and referral to gifted programs. They also have control over the culture of the classroom and to what extent diverse ideas and opinions are welcomed or shunned. Of course, the quality of instruction also rests with educators. More formal mentors from the community can direct gifted students to career opportunities, model appropriate social roles and responsibilities, and open doors to future opportunities that may not be available otherwise (Hébert, 2002). Mentoring relationships that work best are often serendipitous and not assigned as part of a course placement or forced option.

Families are partners in education and play a significant role in developing the intrapersonal skills of gifted CLD learners. Talent development research suggests that family support directly influences to what extent a raw talent is developed and recognized (Bloom, 1985; Csikszentmihalyi et al., 1993). Family support of educational endeavors will go a long way in optimizing learning experiences and supporting talent (VanTassel-Baska, 1989).

Counselors, both in and out of school, are extremely influential in teaching coping strategies as well as enhancing career opportunities for CLD students. Counselors in schools with high numbers of disadvantaged students may be less equipped to guide college choice or encourage the application to premier universities (Wyner, Bridgeland, & DiIulio, 2007). In many high-poverty schools, counselors are the first to be given added responsibilities or to be released if there are budget cuts, thus minimizing the support needed to help CLD students achieve. Programs such as those sponsored by the Jack Kent Cooke Foundation or the Schuler Family Foundation provide mentoring and career counseling for high-ability CLD students to achieve and have enjoyed high rates of students' application, acceptance, and graduation from major universities as a result.

Curriculum, instruction, and student internal and external support systems are important to the overall success of the CLD gifted learner and his or her future achievements. How, then, do educators work to develop a curricular program to best meet the intrapersonal, academic, and cultural needs of CLD learners?

INTERNAL FACTORS THAT IMPACT STUDENT ACHIEVEMENT

Intrapersonal factors and external supports cannot be overlooked, as these also play an important role in the lives of gifted CLD students and contribute to the extent to which they achieve. Borland, Schnur, and Wright (2000) studied five gifted minority students from Harlem and recorded higher student academic achievement when they were identified early and given appropriate academic opportunities. Even though early identification was key, the researchers noted that intrapersonal skills and family support structures also played important roles in student career paths and life choices. Worrell and colleagues (2001) conducted a

9-year national database study and concurred that psychosocial variables were more likely to contribute to CLD learners' participation in ongoing talent development than their grade point average or achievement scores.

Although limited studies have been conducted to determine the specific effects of precollegiate programming on psychosocial and intrapersonal skills of gifted CLD learners (Stambaugh, 2007b), self-concept and efficacy seem to be two important factors that contribute to their overall success. In a study of social support and self-concept of students in a summer gifted program, VanTassel-Baska, Olszewski-Kubilius, and Kulieke (1994) noted minimal differences between ethnic and gender groups, but significant differences between high and low socioeconomic students. Disadvantaged students had a lower academic and social efficacy concept than their wealthier peers (VanTassel-Baska et al., 1994). Other contributing factors included achievement motivation and coping mechanisms of these students (VanTassel-Baska, 1989). Students who are motivated and have the tools to achieve and cope with the adversities of life are more likely to perform better than those of similar backgrounds without the skills. Although there is extensive literature in the psychology field focused on the development of efficacy, motivation, and positive self-concept, there is little research specific to the development of these skills in gifted CLD learners. More research on internal and external factors that impact learning and their relationship to curriculum development is needed.

CHAPTER 5

Next Steps: An Evidence-Based Model for Curriculum Development and Adaptation

A model for curriculum design and adaptation was created to synthesize the information gathered from the known information discussed in this book. Figure 9 illustrates this conceptual model, which includes three main parts: the curriculum, the instructional environment, and the student. Each part is further explained.

THE CURRICULUM

When developing curriculum for gifted CLD learners, there are three core components to be included as part of the actual curriculum: models and organizers for scaffolding of tasks, relevant task demands and activities, and higher order thinking and problem-solving tasks embedded within a particular discipline or content domain. Scaffolding is shown within the curriculum through the use and breakdown of models used by experts. Examples of scaffolding models within the research-based programs are evidenced in a variety of ways. Some examples from the curriculum projects discussed in Chapter 2 include Project Clarion's Wheel of Scientific Investigation, which provides a model for how scientists think in an organized way; M3's hint and think deeply cards; and Jacob's Ladder and Project U-STARS~Plus, both of which guide students from lower to higher level thinking.

Relevance in a curriculum is evidenced by connections to the world of the student. These connections can be simulated as part of an experience that is created in lieu of access, or can include real connections to

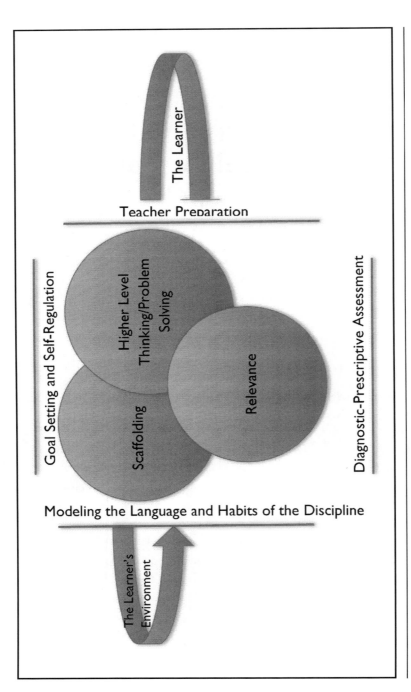

Figure 9. A model of curriculum development and instruction for CLD learners. From Stambaugh (2010).

the students' circumstance, environment, or culture as a primary way to help the student connect with the content being taught. Examples of relevance in the projects described in Chapter 2 include SEM-R's interest-based books from which students could self-select a meaningful book linked to their life, connections to contrived school situations to teach scientific processes and content in the students' school environment as illustrated in several units from Project Clarion, and the problem-based science units from Project Breakthrough.

Higher order thinking skills and problem-solving opportunities comprise the third feature of the curriculum design. Although some may assume this feature is just a natural component of any curriculum for the gifted, many CLD learners do not have opportunities to practice higher level thinking skills—especially if not identified as gifted or in a school that selects remedial, skill-based curriculum without the added dimension of higher order thinking or problem-solving features. All of the curriculum studies discussed in Chapter 2 included higher order thinking skills within the discipline as the primary hallmark of the curriculum. Although these skills may need to be scaffolded or made relevant for the learner to comprehend, they are necessary for student growth. Several of the researchers from the projects reported that many teachers did not believe that the students could perform at the expected levels outlined in the curriculum, but after some professional development and encouragement to teach the more rigorous curriculum, teachers were raising expectations of CLD learners and allowing more opportunities for them to show their unique abilities and gifts. When all three of these curriculum components are featured together in one unit or lesson, CLD learners are more likely to be engaged and show greater learning gains.

THE INSTRUCTIONAL ENVIRONMENT

As noted in Figure 9, the curriculum for CLD learners cannot stand alone; it is impacted and framed by key instructional features that teachers or principals must adhere to if the curriculum is to have a positive impact. First is teacher preparation. Every successful project studied that positively impacted gifted CLD learners' achievement and well-being focused on teacher preparation as a key feature of the project. This preparation includes but is not limited to modeling of curriculum components, awareness of the characteristics of gifted CLD learners, and ongoing monitoring, feedback, problem solving, and communication about the curriculum and instructional process of the intervention. Professional development within a school insinuates that teachers are learners and that the curriculum is important enough to discuss in a formal setting. Moreover, professional development is necessary if a positive and healthy learning environment for gifted CLD learners is to be actualized and more CLD learners who are underserved can have opportunities to show their talents in ways that teachers recognize.

Next, diagnostic/prescriptive instruction is another hallmark of a healthy instructional environment that celebrates learning of all students regardless of the differences in ethnicity or ability. Most of the projects shared in Chapter 2 incorporated some type of pre- and postassessment, not only to measure student gains but to help teachers determine the strengths and needs of their students so that the curriculum can be better matched to the CLD learners' needs. If the curriculum itself is scaffolded, then teachers can immediately use the preassessment to match the student to the appropriate curriculum task demands, activities, or models.

Teacher modeling of thinking processes and the habits of the expert within a particular discipline is another feature of a learning environment that celebrates achievement and ultimately shows growth in students' learning. This modeling is illustrated in Project Athena through the teaching of persuasive writing and the analysis of writing products as aligned with the model. M3 focused on modeling through the explanation of mathematical thinking journals and mathematical vocabulary. SEM-R used guided discussions and reading groups as a way for teachers to model literary thinking.

Goal setting and student self-monitoring is the final component of a healthy learning environment and is evidenced in a variety of ways. Many CLD learners, especially those of poverty, have a difficult time with self-regulation and the setting of long-term goals. An instructional environment that allows students to become partners in their own learning can enhance student motivation and subsequent learning and achievement. The SEM-R teachers provided goal-setting opportunities so that students could determine the number of minutes they would spend reading independently. As such, the students outperformed their peer counterparts in the amount of time reading and their interest in reading increased. Other projects incorporated goal setting and self-monitoring through long-term independent study projects with short-term accountability and teacher guidance.

THE STUDENT

One cannot plan a relevant curriculum or an engaging learning environment without knowing the learner. This "knowing" goes beyond interest and learning style inventories and is impacted by the internal and external factors the learner possesses. These factors circle the model in Figure 9, as they are integral to everything that goes on the classroom, and the classroom impacts these factors. They are cyclic and linked. Educators must be aware of the students' culture, background, and levels of access if a relevant curriculum is to be designed or adapted. Moreover, teachers must understand how to build in small successes through scaffolding for students with lower self-esteem or struggles with efficacy. In addition, environments beyond the school day can be sought to enhance the school experience and provide access to learning and acceleration.

CHAPTER 6

Implications for Practice and School Reform

What are the practical applications to consider when providing and/ or designing curriculum and instruction for CLD gifted learners? The following ideas may be used as a guide for key stakeholders to optimize talent and educational opportunity.

Educators should do the following:

- Deliberately select research-based curriculum that provides scaffolding through questioning and thinking models, acceleration with support, and opportunities for real-world projects and problem solving. If educators are not in a position philosophically or financially to incorporate research-based curriculum, they can apply pedagogical strategies and key components of research-based curriculum (as previously discussed) as part of a differentiated curriculum.

- Model communication techniques and metacognitive skills. Appropriate scaffolding of dialogue and metacognitive thinking will equip CLD students with ways to express ideas creatively in the language of the discipline and learn how to think through situations by applying multiple perspectives and resources. The modeling must be deliberate and consistent in working with CLD students.

- Ensure that the curriculum intervention matches the identification methods used to admit gifted CLD learners into special programs. There is nothing more discouraging than being thrust into an accelerated program that does not match one's unique abilities. Unfortunately, too many times students are admitted to gifted programs by nonverbal measures but are forced to engage in advanced verbal activities that do not match their strengths (and vice versa). Special gifted education programs must be differentiated as well.

- Cultivate a classroom climate that promotes diversity of ideas and opinions. This is accomplished through teacher modeling, open-ended questions, support of varying ideas and opinions, solicitation of multiple ideas and perspectives, promotion of cooperation and respect in self and others, and acceptance of all students regardless of ethnicity or socioeconomic status. Teachers should become aware that they may be viewing the world through a different cultural or socioeconomic lens—one that might be quite different from that of their students. Teachers should learn about the cultures and backgrounds of their CLD students and plan curriculum and instruction accordingly.

- Set appropriately high expectations and provide support. As discovered in many of the curriculum projects discussed, CLD students can work at much higher levels of cognition than anticipated if they are provided early support and scaffolding before being moved into advanced work without preparation. It is better to provide a more accelerated curriculum for CLD learners with appropriate scaffolding, if necessary, than to aim low and then realize too late that students are capable of much more— yet were not provided the appropriate opportunities and access to advanced opportunities and curriculum. Students will never perform at advanced skill levels if they are always kept working at lower levels due to teacher misperceptions about CLD or disadvantaged students' capabilities.

- Choose curriculum materials that include characters, examples, and situations related to the cultures of CLD students in the classroom. It is important for students to see themselves reflected in the materials used in the gifted education program. In language arts, in particular, there are many books that feature children from diverse cultures. In other subjects, contemporary textbook authors have made an attempt to feature diverse ethnic and cultural perspectives. Teachers can enlist the assistance of the library media specialist or content-area curriculum experts to help find appropriate materials.

- Assess growth in a variety of ways. Be wary of applying only one method of measurement for student achievement. Just as gifted CLD students need a different approach to curriculum, they also need a variety of opportunities to show their knowledge. Combining varied standardized assessments at different key stages of development, curriculum-based pre- and postmeasures, and ongoing formative assessment will provide teachers with the information necessary to make good judgments about their students' abilities.

School counselors should do the following:

- Learn about the characteristics and needs of gifted CLD students, particularly their social-emotional needs. Counselors can take a graduate-level course, attend gifted education workshops, or read one of the books suggested in Appendix B at the end of this publication. Because the topic of gifted education is rarely covered in basic teacher training, and even less so in counselor training, it is important for counselors to add this information to their repertoire. School counselors may be called upon to serve as a resource to administrators, a buffer between teachers and parents, and an advocate for gifted students.
- Learn about the specific cognitive, psychological, and affective characteristics of CLD gifted students. After familiarizing themselves about the general needs of gifted learners, counselors should then focus on CLD students, particularly the populations of students served in their school setting. Learn about specific counseling needs that CLD students may have, such as those discussed in Chapter 4 of this book.
- Provide individual and small-group sessions for students on goal setting and time management. This is important for focusing on affective as well as cognitive development. It may also be helpful to provide short sessions for parents in order for them to

facilitate the child's work at home. Teaching students and their parents how to reflect upon student learning and articulate ideas by thinking in a metacognitive way will enhance a student's ability to self-monitor.

- Develop a mentorship program for CLD students. The purpose of the program could be to promote motivation and interest in a discipline or to provide a good academic role model. At the elementary level, this can be informal and can be handled within the school setting. For secondary students, the mentorship could be more formal and could involve some time outside the school building. Many community organizations have individuals who are interested in mentoring students; this provides a wonderful opportunity to utilize community support and to provide value-added experiences for CLD students.

- Find resources for teachers to facilitate their work with CLD students. These resources could include books about eminent individuals who would be considered CLD, movies about individuals who are CLD and have been successful in the school setting, guest speakers to provide career guidance, and special programs for gifted students. Keep in mind that teachers may want a counselor's assistance when trying techniques like bibliotherapy (use of books to address behavioral or emotional issues) or cinematherapy (use of movie clips to address behavioral or emotional issues); specific information about these techniques can be found in the gifted education literature. School counselors should work collaboratively with classroom teachers and use counseling techniques to assist CLD students.

Educational leaders, including building administrators and central office gifted education coordinators, should do the following.

- Provide professional development about gifted CLD students' characteristics and effective curriculum and instructional techniques for this population on an ongoing basis to all faculty and paraprofessionals. Most teachers are unaware of the special needs of this population. All of the projects reviewed earlier in this book emphasized professional development as a key component.

The professional development should be ongoing and built into the school improvement plan.

- Include gifted CLD learners' achievement as a criterion in teacher evaluation and accountability measures. The adage "what gets measured, gets done" is true in this scenario. If teachers know they are accountable for providing differentiated instruction based on best practices and will be evaluated as a result, they are more likely to focus on strategies that enhance student learning—especially if these scores are disaggregated for planning.

- Provide targeted course options for CLD students in their areas of strength. These options, designed to focus on specific academic talents, should provide acceleration and the appropriate level of challenge for the learners (MacFarlane & Feng, 2010).

- Encourage a welcoming school community that celebrates the individual child. In schools with large populations of English language learners (ELL), for example, an excellent opportunity for cultural understanding is possible through learning about their native cultures. Viewing students who speak fluently in their native language and are working on English (i.e., on track to become bilingual) as having a strength rather than a weakness is an example of the "at potential" mindset (Coleman et al., 2007).

- Be aware of and enlist the help of the community supports that exist for CLD students. Provide information for parents about these support systems. Invite individuals from community groups to participate in school PTA meetings or other gatherings. The school personnel must serve as a conduit for connecting parents with community supports such as civic groups and local agencies (Swanson, 2010).

- Select curriculum and/or curriculum models that are known to be effective with high-ability CLD learners. Even if the curriculum materials that are commercially available do not fit well with the district or state curriculum, they may be adapted or used as models for what should be done.

- Encourage career counseling and mentorships as part of student development. These emphases should be started in the elementary grades, providing students with exposure to positive role models and professionals working in the areas of interest.

- Involve families of CLD gifted learners as educational partners. Provide professional development opportunities for them and include family nights where they can work on activities with their child. Spend time with parents showing them how to work with their children on higher level skills.
- Use a variety of strategies to increase communication and interaction with parents:
  - Provide transportation to school events.
  - Disseminate information in multiple languages.
  - Provide translators for meetings and conferences.
  - Solicit parents to serve as volunteers or to provide leadership in school activities.
  - Hold parent meetings outside of the school setting, such as in neighborhood churches or local bookstores. This may help parents to feel safer, plus it also will allow them to bring younger children with them. Provide opportunities for their involvement in the educational process on their "timeframes and turfs" (Swanson, 2010, p. 150).

- Develop a parent network to help monitor the progress of targeted CLD students.
  - Use the network as a way to encourage sustained parental involvement.
  - Find positive role models for CLD students from within the network.
  - Use parents to help monitor English language development.

Researchers should do the following, based on findings from *Overlooked Gems* (VanTassel-Baska & Stambaugh, 2007a), a national conference on promising students of poverty that outlined a research agenda for this special population:

- Conduct research regarding the effects of curriculum and instructional approaches commonly found in gifted education programs using CLD promising learners as the target population. Study which interventions are most effective for this population.

- Determine the differences between ethnicity and poverty and how each impacts CLD learners.
- Design research studies that will provide teachers and administrators with specific information about the efficacy of various curricula.
- Conduct research about school and family factors that support or detract from English fluency.
- Develop research studies about the efficacy of various professional development delivery models, specifically as they relate to gifted education pedagogy.
- Collect longitudinal data regarding value-added programs for CLD students, including factors that contribute to their talent development.

Policy makers should do the following:

- Include gifted CLD learners as a subgroup on state report card measures. Also, disaggregate results by poverty and ethnicity level within the subgroups as well as overall. These data can be used as support for garnering additional resources or for maintaining current resource levels.
- Know the research that impacts these students and develop and enact policies accordingly. Data supporting the proposed policy will be crucial for getting support for the enactment of a policy. For example, there are various types of policies based on research that are related to the acceleration of students. Policy makers should use the research data and these existing policies as a basis for developing their own policy.
- Create general educational policies that do not contradict or inhibit gifted CLD learners' needs. An unintended consequence of some efforts to "raise the bar" has been the development of rigid expectations that do not account for student differences in readiness or how they demonstrate what they have learned. The current high-stakes testing environment is one in which all students are typically expected to demonstrate their knowledge in

the same manner. This situation may not be in the best interest of CLD students, whose learning preferences may indicate that they need to respond in a different manner than what the state testing policy involves.

- Be prepared to plan for the monitoring and assessment of any new policy. All stakeholders, such as parents, legislators, and administrators, will expect to see data related to the implementation of the policy (Lord, 2010). In developing the policy, then, a key task should be to include provisions for monitoring and evaluation as a component.

- Examine existing policies to determine how they hinder or facilitate CLD learners' participation and success in gifted education programs. Paradoxical or rigid policies may possibly result in CLD students being exited from the gifted program. For example, a policy that requires a student to maintain a certain grade point average in all subjects could be detrimental to a CLD student who has a single primary strength area but who is generally weak in other subjects.

- Understand that policies must be explicit in addressing the needs of CLD students (Castellano, 2011). A policy should exist that advocates for the inclusion of CLD students in gifted education programs. Additionally, district policies should have specific language that relates to identification, assessment, and service options for CLD students in gifted education programs. Although many would argue that policy language is meant to be vague, it is essential that there is specificity when addressing provisions for CLD students so that they are guaranteed to be included in gifted programs.

- Remember that policy work "requires a broad, dedicated, and committed leadership network" (Lord, 2010, p. 261). This network should include members of the state affiliate for gifted education, faculty and staff from higher education institutions, and strong advocates for gifted education. A deliberate effort must be made to cultivate relationships and build this leadership network that can provide resources and data for helping school districts and state education agencies develop policies benefiting CLD students.

Professional development coordinators in gifted education should do the following:

- Share the results of research about curriculum efficacy for CLD learners with teachers and administrators. Teachers need to understand that the research findings have driven the development and modification of the curriculum interventions discussed in this book. It is important to describe the relationship of the research to what should be done in the classroom in an explicit manner. Use the model presented here, which is based on a synthesis of multiple research studies, as part of the best practices for teaching CLD learners and creating or adapting curriculum and instructional opportunities for them.
- Learn about the characteristics and needs of CLD gifted students. Include this information in workshops focusing on at-risk groups of students. Refer to the NAGC-CEC Knowledge and Skill Standards for Gifted and Talented Education (NAGC & CEC, 2006); there are multiple standards that relate either directly or indirectly to working with CLD students. Attempting to improve the cultural competency of teachers through targeted professional development may enhance teachers' awareness of the characteristics and needs of CLD students (MacFarlane & Feng, 2010).
- Help teachers understand their biases and assumptions about students of various races and socioeconomic statuses. Use cinematherapy, case studies, action research, and book studies of eminent people who would be considered CLD to help illustrate the information to teachers (Swanson, 2010). The time spent on this aspect must be emphasized; if teachers continue to harbor prejudices or hold preconceived notions about certain groups of people, it will be difficult for them to make the modifications necessary for identifying and serving CLD students.
- Include guided practice for teachers in the pedagogy of gifted education. They need time to explore the teaching models and

see how they work. Make the connection between learner characteristics and curricular modifications explicit to the participants. It is essential for teachers to add curricular approaches and instructional methods that address the strengths and preferences of these students (Swanson, 2010). If possible, have teachers practice the pedagogy in their classrooms, then return for a debriefing session to discuss what was successful and what did not work with actual students.

- Encourage district or school personnel to establish ongoing, sustained professional development sessions. A single training session is insufficient for teachers to learn about the complex topic of CLD students. Sessions about the characteristics and needs of CLD students and related curricular modifications should be provided for all personnel who are charged with working with these students. As part of the professional development, teachers should try the modifications, be observed, and then be given targeted feedback.

- Explain the unique characteristics and subsequent modifications for gifted CLD learners. Whether providing professional development targeted toward the general population or that specific to CLD learners or gifted students, help educators understand the unique needs of this group and ways to modify curriculum that may be different than the regular population. Scaffolding (why and how) is an essential component that should be the focus of this training.

Parents should do the following:
- Become partners with the school so that they can advocate more effectively for their child. This means being visible at all types of school events, including conferences, PTA meetings, and school programs. Parents should take advantage of seminars and other programs offered at their child's school to expand their own knowledge base.

- Encourage their child to advocate for him- or herself. Parents should teach their child how to discuss his or her needs with the teacher in a respectful manner. It may be helpful to role-play with the child. Parents can pretend to be the teacher and have their child make a request for help to them, just as he or she would do when talking to the teacher.

- Ask for help when needed. If language is a barrier, parents should find someone who can help them to communicate effectively with their child's teacher. If parents find a special activity that might be beneficial to their child, they should ask about scholarship opportunities and transportation if needed.
- Educate others about their child's unique needs. Attend parent conferences to ensure that the teacher is aware of the child's strengths and weaknesses. Parents can teach others about their beliefs and values, including how those intersect or conflict with school values.
- Serve as a volunteer in the child's school. There are many opportunities to assist in a school, such as serving on PTA committees, volunteering for cafeteria or playground duty, chaperoning field trips, and working at an event. This shows that parents are interested in helping the school, and it also shows their child in a visible way that parents work hand in hand with the school for the benefit of children.

Community members should do the following:
- Volunteer their services at a neighborhood school, such as translating, tutoring, and mentoring. There are many needs in America's schools. Volunteers may be able to contribute a service not provided for in the budget, possibly assisting CLD students.
- Share their profession with students who have shown talent in certain related skill areas. At the elementary level, community members can speak at career day events or serve as a guest speaker in classrooms. At the secondary level, community members can offer their job site as a possible place for internships.
- Share resources and time with local school leaders if they are a member of a community organization or a business that can provide support for CLD students. Sometimes the school personnel are unaware of some of the agencies/organizations that are available to assist students outside the school setting.

CONCLUSION

Curriculum approaches for advanced CLD learners must be deliberate and targeted to the needs of this special group. Curriculum must be relevant to the students' lives and feature advanced-level thinking skills with modeling and scaffolding embedded so that students have opportunities to think critically, apply advanced levels of thinking to meaningful tasks, and practice using the language of the discipline. Teachers should model thinking and metacognitive practices. Pre- and postassessments should be used to plan for student learning and to measure growth and progress. Although curriculum is important, other factors must also be considered for CLD high-ability students to succeed, including opportunities for career counseling, development of intrapersonal skills, and connections with supportive individuals who are willing to mentor them in content and social skills.

References

Baldwin, A. Y. (1994). The seven plus story: Developing hidden talent among students in socioeconomically disadvantaged environments. *Gifted Child Quarterly, 38,* 80–84.

Baldwin, A. Y. (2007). The untapped potential for excellence. In J. VanTassel-Baska & T. Stambaugh (Eds.), *Overlooked gems: A national perspective on low-income promising learners* (pp. 23–25). Washington, DC: National Association for Gifted Children.

Banks, J. A. (1997). Multicultural education: Characteristics and goals. In J. A. Banks & C. A. M. Banks (Eds.), *Multicultural education: Issues and perspectives* (3rd ed., pp. 3–31). Boston, MA: Allyn & Bacon.

Banks, J. A. (2004). Multicultural education: Historical development, dimensions, and practices. In J. A. Banks & C. A. M. Banks (Eds.), *Handbook of research on multicultural education* (2nd ed., pp. 3–29). San Francisco, CA: Jossey-Bass.

Baum, S., & Owen, S. (2004). Talent beyond words: Identification of potential talent in dance and music in elementary students. In E. Zimmerman (Ed.), *Artistically and musically talented students* (pp. 57–72). Thousand Oaks, CA: Corwin Press.

Bloom, B. S. (Ed.). (1985). *Developing talent in young people.* New York, NY: Ballantine.

Bomer, R., Dworin, J. E., May, L., & Semingson, P. (2008). Miseducating teachers about the poor: A critical analysis of Ruby Payne's claims about poverty. *Teachers College Record, 110,* 2497–2531.

Boothe, D., & Stanley, J. C. (Eds.). (2004). *In the eyes of the beholder: Critical issues for diversity in gifted education.* Waco, TX: Prufrock Press.

Borland, J. H. (1989). *Planning and implementing programs for the gifted.* New York, NY: Teachers College Press.

Borland, J. H., Schnur, R., & Wright, L. (2000). Economically disadvantaged students in a school for the academically gifted: A postpositivist inquiry into individual and family adjustment. *Gifted Child Quarterly, 44,* 13–32.

Bracken, B. A., VanTassel-Baska, J., Brown, E. F., & Feng, A. (2007). Project Athena: A tale of two studies. In J. VanTassel-Baska & T. Stambaugh (Eds.), *Overlooked gems: A national perspective on low-income promising learners* (pp. 63–67). Washington, DC: National Association for Gifted Children.

Brewer, E. (2005). A longitudinal study of the talent search program. *Journal of Career Development, 31,* 195–208.

Briggs, C. J. (2003). *Exemplary interventions and practices that develop the gifts and talents of culturally, linguistically, and ethnically diverse students* (Unpublished doctoral dissertation). University of Connecticut, Storrs.

Briggs, C. J., & Renzulli, J. S. (2009). Scaffolding CLED students to promote greater participation in programs for the gifted and talented. *Journal of Urban Education: Focus on Enrichment, 6,* 1–15.

Callahan, C. M. (2005). Identifying gifted students from underrepresented populations. *Theory Into Practice, 44,* 98–105.

Campbell, F. A., & Ramey, C. T. (1990). The relationship between Piagetian cognitive development, mental test performance, and academic achievement in high-risk students with and without early educational experience. *Intelligence, 14,* 293–308.

Canivez, G. L., & Konold, T. R. (2001). Assessing differential prediction bias in the Developing Cognitive Abilities Test across gender, race/ethnicity, and socioeconomic groups. *Educational and Psychological Measurement, 61,* 159–171.

Castellano, J. A. (2011). Cultural competency: Implications for educational and instructional leaders in gifted education. In J. A. Castellano & A. D. Frazier (Eds.), *Special populations in gifted educa-*

tion: Understanding our most able students from diverse backgrounds (pp. 383–400). Waco, TX: Prufrock Press.

Center for Gifted Education. (2010). *Budding botanists.* Waco, TX: Prufrock Press.

Center for Gifted Education. (1999). *Guide to teaching a language arts curriculum for high-ability learners.* Williamsburg, VA: Author.

Coleman, M. R. (2007). Rejecting the stereotype: Project U-STARS~Plus assumes "at potential." *Early Developments, 11*(2), 12–15.

Coleman, M. R., Coltrane, S. S., Harradine, C., & Timmons, L. A. (2007). Impact of poverty on promising learners, their teachers, and their schools. *Journal of Urban Education: Focus on Enrichment, 6,* 59–67.

College of William and Mary, Center for Gifted Education. (2007). *Electricity city: Student pack.* Dubuque, IA: Kendall Hunt.

College of William and Mary, Center for Gifted Education. (1999). *Electricity city: Creating a city's electrical system.* Dubuque, IA: Kendall Hunt.

Csikszentmihalyi, M., Rathunde, K., & Whalen, S. (1993). *Talented teenagers: The roots of success and failure.* Cambridge, UK: Cambridge University Press.

Education Trust. (2005). *The funding gap 2005: Low-income and minority students shortchanged by most states.* Washington, DC: Author.

Ford, D. Y. (1995). Desegregating gifted education: A need unmet. *Journal of Negro Education, 64,* 52–62.

Ford, D. Y. (2011). *Multicultural gifted education* (2nd ed.). Waco, TX: Prufrock Press.

Ford, D. Y., & Harris, J. J. (1999). *Multicultural gifted education.* New York, NY: Teacher's College Press.

Ford, D. Y., Howard, T. C., Harris, J. J., & Tyson, C. A. (2000). Creating culturally responsive classrooms for gifted African American students. *Journal for the Education of the Gifted, 23,* 397–427.

FPG Child Development Institute. (2010, July). Rejecting the "at-risk" stereotype: Project U-STARS~Plus helps kids "at-potential." *FPG Snapshot, 61.* Retrieved from http://www.fpg.unc.edu/~snapshots/Snap61_USTARS.PDF

Frasier, M. M. (1991). Disadvantaged and culturally diverse gifted students. *Journal for the Education of the Gifted, 14,* 234–245.

Gavin, M. K., Casa, T. M., Adelson, J. L., Carroll, S. R., & Sheffield, L. J. (2009). The impact of advanced curriculum on the achievement of mathematically promising elementary students. *Gifted Child Quarterly, 53,* 188–202.

Gavin, M. K., Chapin, S., Dailey, J., & Sheffield, L. (2006). *Unraveling the mystery of the moli stone: Place value and numeration.* Dubuque, IA: Kendall Hunt.

Gira, R. (2007). The challenge: Preparing promising low-income students for college. In J. VanTassel-Baska & T. Stambaugh (Eds.), *Overlooked gems: A national perspective on low-income promising learners* (pp. 68–73). Washington, DC: National Association for Gifted Children.

Gorski, P. (2005). *Savage unrealities: Uncovering classism in Ruby Payne's framework.* Retrieved from http://www.edchange.org/publications/Savage_Unrealities.pdf

Hébert, T. P. (2002). Educating gifted children from low socioeconomic backgrounds: Creating visions of a hopeful future. *Exceptionality, 10,* 127–138.

Hébert, T. P., & Beardsley, T. M. (2001). Jermaine: A critical case study of a gifted Black child living in rural poverty. *Gifted Child Quarterly, 45,* 85–103.

Jatko, B. P. (1995). Using a whole class tryout procedure for identifying economically disadvantaged students in three socioeconomically diverse schools. *Journal for the Education of the Gifted, 19,* 83–105.

Johnsen, S., & Ryser, G. (1994). Identification of young gifted children from lower income families. *Gifted and Talented International, 9,* 62–68.

Johnsen, S. K., Feuerbacher, S., & Witte, M. (2007). Increasing the retention of gifted students from low-income backgrounds in university programs for the gifted: The UYP project. In J. VanTassel-Baska (Ed.), *Serving gifted learners beyond the traditional classroom: A guide to alternative programs and services* (pp. 51–81). Waco, TX: Prufrock Press.

Joseph, L. M., & Ford, D. Y. (2006). Nondiscriminatory assessment: Considerations for gifted education. *Gifted Child Quarterly, 50*, 42–53.

Kitano, M. (2007). Poverty, diversity, and promise. In J. VanTassel-Baska & T. Stambaugh (Eds.), *Overlooked gems: A national perspective on low-income promising learners* (pp. 31–35). Washington, DC: National Association for Gifted Children.

Kitano, M. (2010). The role of culture in shaping expectations for gifted students. In J. VanTassel-Baska (Ed.), *Patterns and profiles of promising learners from poverty* (pp. 11–31). Waco, TX: Prufrock Press.

Lohman, D. F. (2005). The role of nonverbal ability tests in identifying academically gifted students: An aptitude perspective. *Gifted Child Quarterly, 49*, 111–138.

Lohman, D. F. (2009). Identifying academically talented students: Some general principles, two specific procedures. In L. V. Shavinina (Ed.), *International handbook of giftedness* (pp. 971–997). Dordrecht, The Netherlands: Springer Science.

Lord, E. W. (2010). Policy and underrepresented gifted students: One state's experience. In J. VanTassel-Baska (Ed.), *Patterns and profiles of promising learners from poverty* (pp. 245–264). Waco, TX: Prufrock Press.

MacFarlane, B., & Feng, A. X. (2010). The patterns and profiles of gifted African American children: Lessons learned. In J. VanTassel-Baska (Ed.), *Patterns and profiles of promising learners from poverty* (pp. 107–128). Waco, TX: Prufrock Press.

Maker, C. J. (1982). *Curriculum development for the gifted.* Rockville, MD: Aspen.

Mantzicopoulos, P. Y. (2000). Can the Brigance K & 1 screen detect cognitive/academic giftedness when used with preschoolers from economically disadvantaged backgrounds? *Roeper Review, 22*, 185–191.

Marland, S. P., Jr. (1972). *Education of the gifted and talented: Report to the Congress of the United States by the U.S. Commissioner of Education and background papers submitted to the U.S. Office of Education, 2 vols* (Government Documents Y4.L 11/2: G36). Washington, DC: U.S. Government Printing Office.

Montgomery, D. (2001). Increasing Native American Indian involvement in gifted programs in rural schools. *Psychology in the Schools, 38*, 467–475.

Naglieri, J. A., & Ford, D. Y. (2003). Addressing underrepresentation of gifted minority children using the Naglieri Nonverbal Ability Test (NNAT). *Gifted Child Quarterly, 47*, 155–160.

National Association for Gifted Children, & Council for Exceptional Children. (2006). *NAGC-CEC teacher knowledge and skill standards for gifted and talented education.* Retrieved from http://www.ncate.org/LinkClick.aspx?fileticket=5zapZLBPUhQ%3D&tabid=676

National Center for Education Statistics. (2006). *The condition of education 2006* (NCES 2006-071). Washington, DC: U.S. Government Printing Office.

New Mexico State Department of Education. (1994). *Technical assistance document—Gifted education.* Albuquerque, NM: Author.

Olszewski-Kubilius, P. (2006). Addressing the achievement gap between minority and nonminority children: Increasing access and achievement through Project EXCITE. *Gifted Child Today, 29*(2), 28–37.

Olszewski-Kubilius, P., & Lee, S. Y. (2004). Parent perceptions of the effects of the Saturday enrichment program on gifted students' talent development. *Roeper Review, 26*, 156–165.

Paul, R. (1990). *Critical thinking: What every person needs to survive in a rapidly changing world.* Rhonert Park, CA: Sonoma State University, Center for Critical Thinking and Moral Critique.

Payne, R. K. (2001). *A framework for understanding poverty.* Highlands, TX: aha! Process.

Plucker, J. A., & Callahan, C. M. (Eds.). (2008). *Critical issues and practices in gifted education: What the research says.* Waco, TX: Prufrock Press.

Plucker, J., Callahan, C. M., & Tomchin, E. M. (1996). Wherefore art thou, multiple intelligences? Alternative assessments for identifying talent in ethnically diverse and economically disadvantaged students. *Gifted Child Quarterly, 40*, 81–92.

Reid, C., Romanoff, B., Algozzine, B., & Udall, A. (2000). An evaluation of alternative screening procedures. *Journal for the Education of the Gifted, 23*, 378–396.

Reis, S. M., McCoach, D. B., Coyne, M., Schreiber, F. J., Eckert, R. D., & Gubbins, E. J. (2007). Using planned enrichment strategies with direct instruction to improve reading fluency, comprehension, and attitude toward reading: An evidence-based study. *The Elementary School Journal, 108*, 3–24.

Renzulli, J. S., & Park, S. (2000). Gifted dropouts: The who and the why. *Gifted Child Quarterly, 44*, 261–272.

Robinson, A., Shore, B. M., & Enersen, D. L. (2007). *Best practices in gifted education: An evidence-based guide*. Waco, TX: Prufrock Press.

Robinson, N. M., Lanzi, R. G., Weinberg, R. A., Ramey, S. L., & Ramey, C. T. (2002). Family factors associated with high academic competence in former Head Start children at third grade. *Gifted Child Quarterly, 46*, 278–290.

Shaunessy, E., Karnes, F. A., & Cobb, Y. (2004). Assessing potentially gifted students from lower socioeconomic status with nonverbal measures of intelligence. *Perceptual and Motor Skills, 98*, 1129–1138.

Shore, B. (1988). *Recommended practices in the education and upbringing of the gifted: A progress report on an assessment of knowledge base*. Indianapolis, IN: Indiana Department of Education, Office of Gifted and Talented Education.

Shumow, L. (1997). Daily experiences and adjustment of gifted low-income urban children at home and school. *Roeper Review, 20*, 35–39.

Sirin, S. R. (2005). Socioeconomic status and academic achievement: A meta-analytic review of research 1990–2000. *Review of Educational Research, 75*, 417–453.

Slocumb, P. D., & Payne, R. K. (2000). *Removing the mask: Giftedness in poverty*. Highlands, TX: RFT Publishing Co.

Sosniak, L. A., & Gabelko, N. H. (2008). *Every child's right: Academic talent development by choice, not chance*. New York, NY: Teachers College Press.

Stambaugh, T. (2007a). *Effects of the Jacob's Ladder Reading Comprehension Program on reading comprehension and critical thinking skills of third, fourth, and fifth grade students in rural, Title I schools* (Doctoral dissertation). Available from ProQuest Dissertations and Theses database. (UMI No. 3254406)

Stambaugh, T. (2007b). Next steps: An impetus for change. In J. VanTassel-Baska & T. Stambaugh (Eds.), *Overlooked gems: A national perspective on low-income promising learners* (pp. 83–88). Washington, DC: National Association for Gifted Children.

Stambaugh, T. (2009, March). *Curriculum features for promising students of poverty.* Presented at the Festschrift for Dr. Joyce VanTassel-Baska, Williamsburg, VA.

Stambaugh, T. (2010, April). *Curriculum and instructional strategies for working with promising students of poverty* [webinar]. Washington, DC: National Association for Gifted Children.

Swanson, J. D. (2006). Breaking through assumptions about low-income, minority gifted students. *Gifted Child Quarterly, 50,* 11–25.

Swanson, J. D. (2010). The patterns and profiles of gifted low-income Caucasian children. In J. VanTassel-Baska (Ed.), *Patterns and profiles of promising learners from poverty* (pp. 129–156). Waco, TX: Prufrock Press.

Taylor, B. M., Pearson, P. D., Clark, K., & Walpole, S. (2000). Effective schools and accomplished teachers: Lessons about primary-grade reading instruction in low-income schools. *The Elementary School Journal, 101,* 121–165.

Title V, Part D. [Jacob K. Javits Gifted and Talented Students Education Act of 1988], Elementary and Secondary Education Act of 1988 (2002), 20 U.S.C. sec. 7253 et seq.

Tivnan, T., & Hemphill, L. (2005). Comparing four literacy reform models in high-poverty schools: Patterns of first-grade achievement. *The Elementary School Journal, 105,* 419–441.

Tomlinson, C. A. (2001). *How to differentiate instruction in mixed-ability classrooms.* Alexandria, VA: Association for Supervision and Curriculum Development.

VanTassel-Baska, J. (1986). Effective curriculum and instructional models for talented students. *Gifted Child Quarterly, 30,* 164–169.

VanTassel-Baska, J. (1989). Case studies of disadvantaged gifted learners. *Journal for the Education of the Gifted, 13,* 22–36.

VanTassel-Baska, J. (1994). *Comprehensive curriculum for gifted learners* (2nd ed.). Boston, MA: Allyn & Bacon.

VanTassel-Baska, J. (2003). *Content-based curriculum for low income and minority gifted learners* (RM03180). Storrs: University of Connecticut, The National Research Center on the Gifted and Talented.

VanTassel-Baska, J. (Ed.). (2010). *Patterns and profiles of promising learners from poverty.* Waco, TX: Prufrock Press.

VanTassel-Baska, J., Feng, A., Brown, E. F., Bracken, B., Stambaugh, T., French, H., . . . Bai, W. (2008). A study of differentiated instructional change over 3 years. *Gifted Child Quarterly, 52,* 297–312.

VanTassel-Baska, J., Johnson, D., & Avery, L. D. (2002). Using performance tasks in the identification of economically disadvantaged and minority gifted learners: Findings from project STAR. *Gifted Child Quarterly, 46,* 110–123.

VanTassel-Baska, J., Olszewski-Kubilius, P., & Kulieke, M. (1994). A study of self-concept and social support in advantaged and disadvantaged seventh and eighth grade gifted students. *Roeper Review, 16,* 186–191.

VanTassel-Baska, J., & Stambaugh, T. (Eds.). (2007a). *Overlooked gems: A national perspective on low-income promising learners.* Washington, DC: National Association for Gifted Children.

VanTassel-Baska, J., & Stambaugh, T. (2007b). *Javits report to the USDOE: Project Clarion research findings.* Presented to the Javits Review Panel, United States Department of Education, Hartford, CT.

VanTassel-Baska, J., & Stambaugh, T. (2008, November). *Project Clarion: Research-based science curriculum for primary students.* Presented at the annual meeting of the National Association for Gifted Children, Tampa, FL.

VanTassel-Baska, J., & Stambaugh, T. (Eds.). (2009a). *Jacob's ladder reading comprehension program: Level 1.* Waco, TX: Prufrock Press.

VanTassel-Baska, J., & Stambaugh, T. (Eds.). (2009b). *Jacob's ladder reading comprehension program: Level 2.* Waco, TX: Prufrock Press.

VanTassel-Baska, J., & Stambaugh, T. (Eds.). (2009c). *Jacob's ladder reading comprehension program: Level 3.* Waco, TX: Prufrock Press.

Westberg, K. L., Archambault, F. X., Jr., Dobyns, S. M., & Salvin, T. J. (1993). *An observational study of instructional and curricular practices used with gifted and talented students in regular classrooms* (RM93104).

Storrs: University of Connecticut, The National Research Center on the Gifted and Talented.

Westberg, K., & Daoust, M. E. (2004). *The results of the replication of the classroom practices survey replication in two states.* Storrs: University of Connecticut, The National Research Center on the Gifted and Talented.

Wigfield, A. (1997). Children's motivation for reading and reading engagement. In J. T. Guthrie & A. Wigfield (Eds.), *Reading engagement: Motivating readers through integrated instruction* (pp. 14–33). Newark, DE: International Reading Association.

Woods, M. B. (2006). *Factors affecting the degree of participation among enrichment program attendees* (Doctoral dissertation). Available from ProQuest Dissertations and Theses database. (UMI No. 3198885)

Worrell, F. C., & Schaefer, B. A. (2004). Reliability and validity of Learning Behaviors Scale (LBS) scores with academically talented students: A comparative perspective. *Gifted Child Quarterly, 48,* 287–309.

Worrell, F. C., Szarko, J. E., & Gabelko, N. H. (2001). Multi-year persistence of non-traditional students in an academic talent development program. *Journal of Secondary Gifted Education, 12,* 80–89.

Wyner, J. S., Bridgeland, J. M., & DiIulio, J. J. (2007). *Achievement trap: How America is failing millions of high-achieving students from lower-income families.* Lansdowne, VA: Jack Kent Cooke Foundation.

Zimmerman, B. (1990). Self-regulated learning and academic achievement: An overview. *Educational Psychologist, 25,* 3–17.

APPENDIX A

Websites and Online Resources

CURRICULUM INTERVENTIONS

The curriculum interventions and projects listed here were discussed in this book. Additional Javits grants projects research briefs and information may be found at the following website: http://www.nagc.org/index.aspx?id=1061.

Mentoring Mathematical Minds (M3)
- Researcher website: http://www.gifted.uconn.edu/projectm3
- Curriculum for Purchase: http://www.kendallhunt.com/m3

The William and Mary Language Arts and Problem-Based Science Units From Project Breakthrough
- Researcher Websites:
  - Science: http://cfge.wm.edu/curr_science.htm
  - Language Arts: http://cfge.wm.edu/athena.htm
  - Articles: http://cfge.wm.edu/research.htm#studies
- Curriculum for Purchase:
  - Language Arts: http://www.kendallhunt.com/cfge_la
  - Science: http://www.kendallhunt.com/cfge_science

The William and Mary Project Clarion Primary Science Units
- Researcher Website: http://cfge.wm.edu/clarion.htm
- Curriculum for Purchase: http://www.prufrock.com

Project U-STARS~Plus
- Researcher Website: No longer available
- Podcast Interview With Researcher: http://www.unc.edu/fpg/fpgvoices/fpgvoices_ustars_nov_2007.mp3
- Curriculum for Purchase: http://www.nagc.org; http://www.cec.sped.org

Jacob's Ladder Reading Comprehension Program
- Researcher Website: http://cfge.wm.edu/curr_language.htm#ladder
- Curriculum for Purchase: http://www.prufrock.com

Schoolwide Enrichment Model-Reading
- Researcher Website: http://www.gifted.uconn.edu/SEMR/index.html
- SEM-R Manual for Purchase: http://www.creativelearningpress.com

TALENT SEARCH PROGRAMS

There are four talent search programs that target different regions of the United States and provide out-of-level testing, reporting, and recognition to high-ability students who choose to participate in the programs. Affiliate organizations of each of the major talent searches may also host programs. Check with major universities for information about program offerings in a specific state.

- Center for Bright Kids Regional Talent Center: http://www.centerforbrightkids.org
- Duke Talent Identification Program (TIP): http://www.tip.duke.edu
- Johns Hopkins University Center for Talented Youth (CTY): http://cty.jhu.edu
- Northwestern Center for Talent Development: http://www.ctd.northwestern.edu

EXTRACURRICULAR OPPORTUNITIES

The following websites provide information on extracurricular opportunities for students.

National Association for Gifted Children (NAGC)

NAGC provides information about extracurricular programs for sponsoring organizations across the nation: http://www.nagc.org/index2.aspx?id=1103.

State Affiliate Websites

Many state gifted organization affiliates may post or know of opportunities available locally. NAGC also hosts a complete listing of state organizations with links to each: http://www.nagc.org/index.aspx?id=609.

Other Organizations and Programs of Interest

- Jack Kent Cooke Foundation: http://www.jkcf.org
- Advancement Via Individual Determination (AVID): http://www.avid.org
- Knowledge Is Power Program: http://www.kipp.org
- Advanced Placement: http://www.collegeboard.com/student/testing/ap/about.html
- International Baccalaureate: http://www.ibo.org

Online Resources for Further Reading and Research Findings

- *Overlooked Gems: A National Perspective on Low-Income Promising Learners*: http://www.nagc.org/uploadedFiles/Publications/Overlooked%20Gems%20(password%20protected%20-%20gifted).pdf
- Davidson Institute: Provides a searchable database of online research articles related to gifted education including special populations: http://www.davidsongifted.org/db/Article/Davidson_Database_Overview_415.aspx

- Jack Kent Cooke Foundation Reports: This website hosts major reports on the status of gifted students of poverty, including those from ethnically diverse backgrounds. Reports listed here include: *No Gifted Child Left Behind, The Achievement Trap, Threading the Needle,* and *Opening Doors*: http://www.jkcf.org/news-knowledge
- National Research Center for Gifted and Talented: This website provides a searchable database of information and research monographs on a variety of topics related to high-ability CLD students: http://www.gifted.uconn.edu/nrcgt.html

APPENDIX B

Annotated Bibliography of Selected Readings by Topic

This annotated bibliography provides additional readings on the topic of disadvantaged populations, including publications not necessarily covered in this book, but of further interest or enhancement on specific topics. The bibliography is divided into four sections: comprehensive information, curriculum and instruction, general factors that contribute to learning, and journal volumes or special editions dedicated to the topic.

COMPREHENSIVE INFORMATION

* Baldwin, A. Y. (Ed.). (2004). *Culturally diverse and underserved populations of gifted students.* Thousand Oaks, CA: Corwin Press.

This book is part of the Essential Readings in Gifted Education series. The 10 articles included in the book are considered to be the seminal ones related to each topic. Articles relate to identification, programming, and the talent development of underserved students. Several case studies of gifted CLD students are given as examples.

* Boothe, D., & Stanley, J. C. (Eds.). (2004). *In the eyes of the beholder: Critical issues for diversity in gifted education.* Waco, TX: Prufrock Press.

Each chapter in this book is dedicated to the needs of diverse populations of gifted students, including issues in gifted education related to race, gender, and socioeconomic status. Chapters include issues such as underachievement and African American students, empowering Hispanic students in gifted education, curriculum compacting as a research-based strategy for diverse students, and talent searches in gifted education.

* Borland, J. (2004). *Issues and practices in the identification and education of gifted students from underrepresented groups*. Storrs: University of Connecticut, The National Research Center on the Gifted and Talented.

This document examines causes of the underrepresentation of economically disadvantaged students, students of color, students from ethnic minorities, and students with limited English proficiency in programs for gifted students. It presents ideas and practices that fall within the range of typical gifted program activities and changes in policy and practice to provide a better education for gifted students.

* Castellano, J. A., & Frazier, A. D. (Eds.). (2011). *Special populations in gifted education: Understanding our most able students from diverse backgrounds*. Waco, TX: Prufrock Press.

This edited book has three different sections pertaining to CLD students: chapters devoted to characteristics and needs of students from diverse backgrounds, chapters focusing on English language learners (ELL), and related issues and topics. The book is a good practical resource for helping educators understand the special populations they may encounter in gifted education classes.

* Plucker, J. A., & Callahan, C. M. (Eds.). (2008). *Critical issues and practices in gifted education: What the research says*. Waco, TX: Prufrock Press.

Critical Issues and Practices in Gifted Education: What the Research Says provides a summary of the research literature related to 50 topics in gifted education. Topics covered include differentiated instruction, identification, mentoring, and other areas relevant to the needs of CLD learners. Included with each summary is a section about practical implications and a list of additional resources.

* Robinson, A., Shore, B. M., & Enersen, D. L. (2007). *Best practices in gifted education: An evidence-based guide.* Waco, TX: Prufrock Press.

This book is divided into three sections, covering 29 practices in gifted education: home, classroom, and school. Each chapter is related to one of the 29 practices and includes a section about what we know and what we can do. Many of the practices pertain to CLD students, such as mentorships, developing talents in culturally diverse learners, and working with promising students from low-income backgrounds.

* VanTassel-Baska, J. (Ed). (2007). *Serving gifted learners beyond the traditional classroom: A guide to alternative programs and services.* Waco, TX: Prufrock Press.

Each chapter in this edited book is devoted to a type of gifted education programming outside the regular school day. Many of the topics are relevant to those working with CLD students: increasing the retention of students from low-income backgrounds in university programs for the gifted, mentorships, and counseling. A summary chart provides a synthesis of the information about each type of alternative program, including longevity, evidence of effectiveness, development of materials specifically for gifted students, and major issues.

VanTassel-Baska, J. (Ed). (2010). *Patterns and profiles of promising learners from poverty.* Waco, TX: Prufrock Press.

Patterns and Profiles of Promising Learners from Poverty covers a variety of topics pertinent to the education of students from low-income families, including the role of culture in education, curriculum for promising learners, psychosocial stressors that affect these learners, professional development for teachers of low-income students, and state policy implementations that affect these students' educations. Chapters look specifically at several types of learners from poverty, including rural and urban-area students, African American students, Caucasian students, and high nonverbal, low verbal students.

CURRICULUM AND INSTRUCTION

* Cunningham, A., Redmond, C., & Merisotis, J. (2003). *Investing early: Intervention programs in selected U.S. states.* Montreal, QC, Canada: Institute for Higher Education Policy.

This report features programs in various states that target Advancement Via Individual Development (AVID) intervention for low-income, first-generation, and minority students in order to get them into the college pipeline. AVID proves to be effective in providing students rigor and support that helps them overcome the negative effects of parents' income and education levels, enabling them to apply for college education.

McKenna, M. A., Hollingsworth, P. L., & Barnes, L. B. (2005). Developing latent mathematics abilities in economically disadvantaged students. *Roeper Review, 27,* 222–227.

This study examined the effects of Kumon instruction, a supplementary, highly sequential, individualized method of developing mathematics skills. Whole classes of Title I elementary school students in grades 2–5 were divided into two groups, those with Kumon instruction and those without. Pre- and posttests were administered to all participants to assess progress, compare standardized test results, and examine levels of acceleration. Results showed that Kumon group students improved their mathematics skill levels more than non-Kumon group students.

* Moon, T. R., & Callahan, C. M. (2001). Curricular modifications, family outreach, and a mentoring program. *Journal for the Education of the Gifted, 24,* 305–321.

This study focused on longitudinal interventions of mentoring, parental involvement, and multicultural curricula on the academic achievement of 273 elementary students from low-socioeconomic environments. The results suggested that the interventions had no statistically significant effect on student achievement in any grade. However, at-risk students were on grade level by the end of the project. In addition, students who participated in the project gained in their problem-solving abilities, creativity, and social skills, and as a result were referred to and placed in gifted programs more often than students who did not receive the project's benefits.

* Olszewski-Kubilius, P. (2006). Addressing the achievement gap between minority and nonminority children: Increasing access and achievement through Project EXCITE. *Gifted Child Today, 29*(2), 28–37.

In this study, data are provided on the achievement of low-income minority students who participated in Project EXCITE, a 5-year intervention program. Results showed that the majority of students who were identified in the third grade and persisted in the program through seventh grade were on track to complete algebra and have significant laboratory science experience prior to high school. Project EXCITE significantly increased the number of minority students, most of whom were also low-income, entering advanced classes in middle school and high school.

Renzulli, J. S., & Reis, S. M. (1994). Research related to the Schoolwide Enrichment Triad Model. *Gifted Child Quarterly, 38*, 7–20.

This article summarizes longitudinal research dealing with categorical components of the Schoolwide Enrichment Triad Model (SEM). Results suggested that the use of this model favorably influences teachers' instructional practices and improves teachers' attitudes toward the education of gifted students and of elementary students' attitudes toward learning and self-concept. The model effectively serves high-ability students in varied educational settings and in schools that serve diverse ethnic and socioeconomic populations.

Schlicter, C. L., & Palmer, W. R. (2002). Talents unlimited: Thinking skills instruction as enrichment for all students. *Research in the Schools, 9,* 53–60.

This article includes a compendium of 30 years of classroom research on the Talents Unlimited model and demonstrates its effectiveness in enhancing creative and critical thinking skills of K–12 students diverse in intellectual ability and achievement, socioeconomic level, and interests. The model includes productive thinking, decision making, planning, forecasting, and communication that students use in creative problem solving. These skills, in concert with academic skills and knowledge, are applied to the curriculum to enrich and enhance students' creative thinking about all areas of instruction.

* VanTassel-Baska, J. (2003). *Content-based curriculum for low income and minority gifted learners* (RM03180). Storrs: University of Connecticut, The National Research Center on the Gifted and Talented.

This monograph and review of the literature addresses planning and developing curricula for low-income and minority gifted learners. Issues discussed include collaboration among professionals working with these students, choice of school program delivery models, involvement of parent and community support systems in nurturing potential, and curriculum interventions directed toward the needs and profiles of this population. Three different sections focus on identification, characteristics, and models and interventions for low-income and minority learners. New directions for future curriculum and program design are discussed.

OTHER FACTORS THAT CONTRIBUTE TO LEARNING

Cross, T., & Burney, V. H. (2005). High ability, rural, and poor: Lessons from Project Aspire and implications for school counselors. *Journal of Secondary Gifted Education, 16,* 148–156.

Project Aspire attempts to increase the number of academically able middle and high school children of poverty by providing them school-based rigorous math and science Advanced Placement (AP) courses through multiple platforms of distance education technologies. This article reported an analysis of the ideas and experiences shared during the training sessions with 21 school counselors. From the analysis and a literature review, the authors offered information for effectively working with high-ability middle and high school students living in rural poverty.

Griffith, J. (1998). The relation of school structure and social environment to parent involvement in elementary schools. *The Elementary School Journal, 99,* 53–81.

This study reported results of parent and student surveys that examined relations among school characteristics and parent involvement. Parents who participated more had a child enrolled in the gifted and talented program, a child in the second grade, multiple children enrolled in the public schools, and perceptions of a safe, empowering, and positive school climate. In contrast, characteristics associated with lower parent participation in school activities included being Hispanic, African American, or Asian American; being of lower socioeconomic status; and having a child enrolled in either special education or the English as a second language program.

* Harmon, D. (2002). They won't teach me: The voices of gifted African American inner-city students. *Roeper Review, 24,* 68–75.

This study examined the effects of busing African American students from a lower income, predominantly minority elementary school to a middle to upper income, predominantly majority elementary school. Students were angry about attending another school, received harassment, were rejected by their White peers, and stayed with their own minority group. They viewed ineffective teachers as having low expectations, lacking in understanding their needs, and providing unfair and unequal treatment. Effective teachers had high expectations, understood the culture, and provided fair and equal treatment.

* Hébert, T. (2002). Educating gifted children from low socioeconomic backgrounds: Creating visions of a hopeful future. *Exceptionality, 10,* 127–138.

The stories of three students from low socioeconomic backgrounds highlight significant issues in educating gifted students living in poverty. Major themes uncovered across the three cases included educators who looked beyond the circumstances of the students and maintained high expectations, the positive influence of enriched teaching-learning opportunities and extracurricular activities, and the success of a mentoring approach with the students.

Hébert, T. P., & Beardsley, T. M. (2001). Jermaine: A critical case study of a gifted black child living in rural poverty. *Gifted Child Quarterly, 45,* 85–103.

In this account of a gifted Black child living in an impoverished rural environment, a university researcher and a classroom teacher collaborated in order to describe a young man's creativity, his resilience, his struggle to find a place for himself in his community, and the significant factors that influenced the early formation of a strong self-identity. The findings of the study offer educators helpful suggestions for identifying and addressing the educational needs of gifted Black children living in rural poverty.

Lubinski, D., & Humphreys, L. G. (1992). Some bodily and medical correlates of mathematical giftedness and commensurate levels of socioeconomic status. *Intelligence, 16,* 99–116.

A survey was conducted on 100,000 high school students to determine the relationship between socioeconomic and health conditions and mathematical giftedness. It was found that physiological well-being is generally more associative with giftedness than socioeconomic advantages. The gifted children's good health may be due to organismic superiority, effective parenting, and other random factors.

Robinson, N. M., Lanzi, R. G., Weinberg, R. A., Ramey, S. L., & Ramey, C. T. (2002). Family factors associated with high academic competence in former Head Start children at third grade. *Gifted Child Quarterly, 46,* 278–290.

Of the 5,400 children in the National Head Start/Public School Early Childhood Transition Demonstration Project tested at the end of third grade, the highest achieving 3% (N = 162) were selected to conduct a principal components analysis on their scores on vocabulary and achievement measures. Compared with the remaining children, the high-achieving children were thriving both socially and academically. The families of these children had somewhat more resources on which to call and somewhat fewer stresses than the families of the other children. Caretakers of high achievers ascribed to more positive parenting attitudes and were seen by teachers as more strongly encouraging their children's progress.

SPECIAL JOURNAL ISSUES RELEVANT TO CLD LEARNERS

Gifted Child Today, Volume 33, Fall 2010

This special issue includes articles dealing specifically with the needs of urban gifted students. It includes information about programs and curriculum and instructional approaches that have been successful with this population.

Journal of Urban Education, Volume 6, Spring 2009.

This special issue is devoted to enrichment for urban students. It includes articles by authorities in gifted education about topics such as the need for scaffolding curriculum and instruction, the underrepresentation of various groups in gifted programs, and issues related to English language learners.

AUTHORS' NOTE

Starred (*) annotations were adapted from VanTassel-Baska, J., & Stambaugh, T. (Eds.). (2007). *Overlooked gems: A national perspective on promising students of poverty*. Washington, DC: National Association for Gifted Children.

About the Authors

Tamra Stambaugh is a research assistant professor of special education and director of Programs for Talented Youth at Vanderbilt University. She is the coauthor of *Comprehensive Curriculum for Gifted Learners* and coeditor of *Overlooked Gems: A National Perspective on Low-Income Promising Students*, the *Jacob's Ladder Reading Comprehension Program* (both with Joyce VanTassel-Baska) and *Leading Change in Gifted Education* (with Bronwyn MacFarlane). Stambaugh has also authored or coauthored journal articles and book chapters on a variety of topics focusing on curriculum, instruction, and leadership. Her research interests include the impact of accelerated curriculum on student achievement, teacher effectiveness, and factors contributing to talent development—especially for students of poverty.

Stambaugh serves as a member of the National Association for Gifted Children professional standards committee. She is the recipient of several awards, including the Margaret The Lady Thatcher Medallion for scholarship, service, and character from The College of William and Mary School of Education. Prior to her appointment at Vanderbilt, she was director of grants and special projects at The College of William and Mary, Center for Gifted Education where she also received her Ph.D. in educational planning, policy, and leadership with an emphasis in gifted education and supervision.

Kimberley L. Chandler is the Curriculum Director at the Center for Gifted Education at The College of William and Mary. In this role, she develops and edits curriculum units for highly able students. She also conducts professional development about gifted education and curriculum development for teachers and administrators in the United States and internationally. Her professional background includes teaching gifted students in a variety of settings, serving as an administrator of a school district gifted program, and working as an Academic Review Team Leader for the Virginia Department of Education. She has also served as an adjunct instructor for gifted education endorsement courses for the University of Virginia, the College of Charleston, Casenex, Inc., and The College of William and Mary. Her research interests include curriculum policy and implementation issues in gifted programs and the design and evaluation of professional development programs for teachers of the gifted.

Chandler completed her Ph.D. in educational policy, planning, and leadership with an emphasis in gifted education administration at The College of William and Mary. As a student, she received the Harry Passow Teacher Scholarship, the Hollingworth Research Award, and the NAGC Outstanding Doctoral Student Award, and was selected for the David L. Clark Graduate Student Research Seminar in Educational Administration and Policy, sponsored by the University Council for Educational Administration. She is a member of the Board of Directors of NAGC, USA Delegate to the World Council for Gifted and Talented Children, and newsletter editor for CEC-TAG.